NOAH'S ARK

Animals In Needlepoint

·

HUGH EHRMAN & ELIZABETH BENN

NOAH'S ARK

Animals In Needlepoint

—•—

HUGH EHRMAN & ELIZABETH BENN

CENTURY

London Sydney Auckland Johannesburg

Also by Hugh Ehrman
Designer Knitting
Designer Needlepoint

Text copyright © Hugh Ehrman 1989
Project photographs copyright © Hugh Ehrman 1989
Artwork copyright © Century Hutchinson 1987
For details of copyright ownership of other illustrations see page 119

Photographs by Julie Fisher
Styling by Jackie Boase
Design by Patrick McLeavey and Sue Storey
Charts by Colin Salmon

First published in 1989 by Century Hutchinson Ltd,
Brookmount House, 62-65 Chandos Place, Covent Garden,
London WC2N 4NW

Century Hutchinson Australia Pty Ltd, 20 Alfred Street,
Milsons Point, Sydney, NSW 2061, Australia

Century Hutchinson New Zealand Limited, PO Box 40-086,
Glenfield, Auckland 10, New Zealand

Century Hutchinson South Africa (Pty) Ltd, PO Box 337,
Bergvlei, 2012 South Africa

Set in Caslon Old Face Roman
Filmset by SX Composing Ltd, Rayleigh, Essex

Printed and bound in Spain by
Printer Industria Grafica SA Barcelona

British Library Cataloguing in Publication Data
Noah's ark: animals in needlepoint.
1. Canvas embroidery. Special subjects. Animals
I. Ehrman, Hugh, *1952* – II. Benn, Elizabeth
746.44'2

ISBN 0-7126-2943-2

CONTENTS

PREFACE

This book was conceived quite simply as a celebration of animals in needlework. It has no party line to preach on either design or technique. It is a varied and miscellaneous collection of needlework designs, in almost every conceivable style, all of which appeal to me in their own individual ways. Three elements hold them together: the subject matter – they all feature animals, fish or birds; Julie Fisher's photography which has been splendidly and originally styled by Jackie Boase throughout; and the text. I was delighted when Elizabeth Benn agreed to write the book. I have known her as long as we have been producing embroidery kits and she seemed just the person to manage a delicate balance between erudition and the light humorous touch that the subject required. She has done so triumphantly and by placing the tapestries in a rough chronological context has produced the framework for this book.

Every year we receive a stream of requests for animal tapestry kits, and not just for the predictable cats and dogs. Pigs, parrots, frogs and fish, sheep, rabbits, ducks and elephants are always in demand, and many more exotic beasts besides. Clearly in a book of this length only a tiny fraction of God's great animal kingdom can be represented, but we decided to make a start.

Far too often the whole subject of animals is treated with an unnecessary sentimentality. As animals become a rarer part of everyday life they assume an air of nostalgia. This is an entirely new development. The decorative arts of previous centuries reveal a world where animals were plentiful, and an essential aspect of both the physical and economic landscape. As a result their depiction in decoration of all types was lively and vital. This book traces the use of animals in the decorative arts, particularly needlework, through the ages giving an historical background to the changing styles. At the same time it shows how many of the designs featured here have been inspired by the styles and themes of the past.

It was a major undertaking to gather together such a body of new work in so short a time. In under six months thirty tapestries had been commissioned and stitched. It was particularly impressive since many of the painters, potters, knitters and embroiderers who contributed work had never designed a tapestry before! This was clearly a gamble but, by sheer good luck, it paid off and the result is a collection of designs that is quite fresh and original. Everyone rose to the occasion and it was great fun putting this book together. All who were involved enjoyed themselves tremendously and I hope you will too. The majority of designs have been charted and all are available as kits.

Hugh Ehrman

INTRODUCTION

Mythological creatures, heraldic beasts, wild and domestic animals have all played a role in the decorative arts throughout the ages — as rampant guardians on the pillars of castle gates, as devoted companions lying under the feet of lords and ladies on medieval tombs, appearing in the corners of portraits, as ceramic ornaments, or as patterns on tapestries, furnishing fabrics and embroideries.

Besotted as we are today with all animals, it is not surprising that they should be such popular subjects for needlework designs. The phenomenon is not new. Since the Bayeux Tapestry was made in the twelfth century animals have appeared in embroidery. Admittedly, they have always taken second place to flowers but then there is a recognized affinity between gardening and embroidery. Keen gardeners who turn to embroidery in the winter say it is their 'indoor gardening'.

During the Elizabethan period, Mary Queen of Scots embroidered animals as decorative canvas-work slips to be placed on wall hangings. In the eighteenth century, when furniture began to be upholstered, exotic birds and pastoral scenes with animals were worked for chair seats. The Victorians embroidered sentimental and whimsical dogs and cats on cushions and even copied Landseer paintings in Berlin woolwork.

Styles in clothing change with increasing rapidity whereas those for interior design move at a far slower pace. Embroidery is more in tune with the latter and stylistic changes evolve over many years, often decades — a fact that can cause confusion as to the date a given item was actually made. Many a woman has embarked enthusiastically on a needlework project only to stop, for one reason or another, half-way through, leaving relatives to finish it, anything up to fifty years later.

After the invention of the printing press in the fifteenth century, books served as the main source of embroidery designs right up until the end of the eighteenth century. The lion and leopard and beasts of the forest remained popular for nearly three centuries, before enjoying a come-back during the Gothic revival of the Victorian era. In the 1920s and 1930s fleet-footed deer and panthers were popular. Today, virtually all animals have an appeal and the design influences come from many sources, old and new, as well as from all corners of the globe. The amazing documentary films on television first introduced many of us to the magical world of the animal kingdom and recent campaigns by conservation and environmental pressure groups have made us all far more aware of animals and of their beneficial effect on man.

In this book I have tried to trace the role animals have played in textiles and other visual arts throughout the centuries, with particular reference to those that have inspired the designers of the new embroidery projects. Beginning with the early *mille-fleurs* tapestries, on which Candace Bahouth based her enchantingly beautiful 'Hunting Rug', we move on to the unicorn, griffin and squirrel derived from the early Renaissance embroideries, the Indian elephants and tigers found in Mughal miniature paintings, and the group inspired by naïve or folk art. During Victorian times, animals proliferated in Berlin woolwork to provide often sentimental portraits of cats, dogs and birds and, after this, we arrive finally at the colourful work by leading artists-craftsmen such as Julie Arkell, who works mainly in papier-mâché, and the embroidery designers Lillian Delevoryas, Kaffe Fassett and Sarah Windrum.

The book provides such a rich variety of animals that there is surely something here to tempt every embroiderer to start stitching.

Elizabeth Benn

EARLY TEXTILES

'Instead of all that deadly white the courtyard was now a blaze of colours: glossy chestnut sides of centaurs, indigo horns of unicorns, dazzling plumage of birds, reddy-brown of foxes, dogs and satyrs, yellow stockings and crimson hoods of dwarfs; and the birch-girls in silver, and the beech-girls in fresh, transparent green, and the larch girls in green so bright that it was almost yellow. And instead of the deadly silence the whole place rang with the sound of happy roarings, brayings, yelpings, barkings, squealings, cooings, neighings, stampings, shouts, hurrahs, songs and laughter.'

The Lion, the Witch and the Wardrobe, C. S. Lewis

MEDIEVAL FANTASY
by Margaret Murton

The painting (left) for the Medieval Fantasy design sets the unicorn, falcon and hare among trees, leaves and flowers, framed with a scrolling border pattern of strawberry leaves, flowers and fruit – similar to those used in samplers of the nineteenth century.

The Bayeux Tapestry, probably the earliest piece of needlework with which most of us are familiar, is full of animals — not just the horses carrying soldiers, but hawks and hounds and a great variety of beasts, birds and fishes, which appear in the friezes above and below the main pictorial narrative. This remarkable embroidered hanging, worked in wool threads on linen, depicts events leading up to the Battle of Hastings in 1066, when William, Duke of Normandy, defeated King Harold of England. It provides a unique picture of the military arts (and associated crafts, such as shipbuilding) of the time. The Tapestry is thought to have been made around 1070 by professional embroiderers in Kent, and was probably commissioned by William's brother, Odo, Bishop of Bayeux, and can be seen in Normandy, France.

ANIMALS IN TAPESTRY

The word 'tapestry', applied to the Bayeux work, is of course mis-used as the hanging was not woven but embroidered. The great medieval tapestries would not appear for another three centuries, and it was the fifteenth and sixteenth centuries before the *mille-fleurs* tapestries, bearing the arms of the nobles who owned the magnificent *châteaux* of the Loire Valley, were made in France and Brussels. These superbly detailed woven pictures provided colour and an illusion of warmth in the sparsely furnished medieval castles. Hunting and hawking, necessary sports to fill the larder, were often the subjects of pieces commissioned for domestic settings. Other popular subjects were the labours of the months, allegorical and mythological themes, and heraldic devices. Scenes from the Old and New Testaments and the lives of the saints were woven for churches.

Among the most beautiful of all medieval tapestries are those in the style known as *mille-fleurs* ('a thousand flowers'), which were made in the late fifteenth and early sixteenth centuries, probably in the Loire Valley. The two best-known series of

mille-fleurs tapestries feature the unicorn, a legendary animal important in medieval Christianity as a symbol of chastity. Both series demonstrate a love of nature and are filled not only with trees and the characteristic profusion of flowers but also with birds, rabbits, monkeys, dogs, foxes, lions and deer.

The 'Lady with the Unicorn' series, in the Cluny Museum, Paris, represents the senses in a highly stylized manner, whereas three of the scenes in the 'Hunt of the Unicorn', in The Cloisters (Metropolitan Museum of Art, New York), with huntsmen and dogs, are more lively and naturalistic. The detail in both series of tapestries is incredibly fine.

The enigmatic sixth tapestry in the 'Lady with the Unicorn' series, which is entitled 'My Sole Desire', provided the inspiration for the Hunting Rug embroidery by Candace Bahouth, shown on page 13.

'Peasants Hunting Rabbits with Ferrets' (*c.* 1450-75, Franco-Burgundian) is just one of a fine group of early tapestries to be found in the Burrell Collection, in Glasgow. It is packed full of humour: men are strategically poised over rabbit holes with round nets; dogs peer anxiously forward; and at the top a woman is handing one of the men a ferret to be put down a run. Meanwhile, at the bottom of the picture a rabbit is hopping along out of sight, followed by her young.

Another tapestry in the Burrell shows exotic animals, such as lions and monkeys intermingled with camels and horses, processing through the streets of Antwerp. 'The Camel Caravan' is believed to be based on an actual procession that took place in Antwerp in 1502, after Vasco da Gama's voyages to the East Indies.

This type of fine workmanship was highly prized, and tapestries were presented by princes and nobles as lavish gifts, as well as bribes in diplomatic negotiations.

Possibly the most remarkable of all the surviving hangings from the late Middle Ages is the

THE ARMS OF MIRO

'The Arms of Miro' (right), an early sixteenth-century Franco-Netherlandish mille-fleurs *tapestry, includes many of the animals that have been used as motifs for textiles over the centuries. The shield, with a mirror in the centre, is a punning reference to the name of the owner, Gabriel Miro. This is one of more than 150 tapestries of the late fifteenth and early sixteenth centuries collected by the late Sir William Burrell to be found in the Burrell Collection, Glasgow.*

famous 'apocalypse' series made in 1375-80 for Louis I, Duke of Anjou, based on cartoons by a Flemish artist, Hennequin of Bruges. Originally the set consisted of seven huge hangings, containing a total of perhaps ninety scenes. Seventy of these remain, housed in a special museum at the castle of Angers, in France. They depict scenes from the vision of St John the Evangelist, some of which incorporate an upper level representing Heaven, with angels, and a lower one, representing the Earth, full of a variety of small animals.

OPUS ANGLICANUM

By the mid-thirteenth century, England had become the undisputed centre for ecclesiastical needlework. Known as *opus anglicanum* ('English work'), this ultra-fine embroidery, worked in silk and gold threads, was greatly prized by cathedrals throughout Europe. Although some secular work was probably made in this style, it is the ecclesiastical vestments that have survived.

Professional embroiderers in London and Winchester carried out the *opus anglicanum* work, using designs by leading draughtsmen for religious figures and scenes, some of which included small animals and birds. Minute split stitch in silk was used for detailed faces and hands, with underside couching (in which the couching threads are pulled to the wrong side, so as to be invisible) for larger areas.

The Black Death (1348-9) decimated the population of Europe, and severely disrupted many trades and arts – among them the English broderers' workshops. The high standard of their sophisticated work was never again to be achieved. Thereafter, richer, patterned fabrics, such as velvets and brocades, which did not require so much embroidered decoration, were imported from Italy for ecclesiastical vestments and altar hangings.

continued on page 18

RABBIT CUSHION
by Candace Bahouth

The rabbit (above) is one of the squares taken from the Hunting Rug to be used as a cushion design. The chart for this cushion is on page 14.

HUNTING RUG
by Candace Bahouth

Candace Bahouth enjoys an international reputation as a brilliantly imaginative tapestry weaver. Physically this form of weaving is extremely demanding as the artist has to sit at an upright loom, slowly building up the images. By contrast, Candace has found embroidery on canvas extremely relaxing and, having become interested in the craft through designing for Hugh Ehrman, is now completely smitten by the tapestry bug.

The famous medieval mille-fleurs tapestry 'The Lady and the Unicorn', in the Cluny Museum, Paris, provided the inspiration for the Hunting Rug (right). The tapestry series consists of allegories of the five senses revolving around the lady, the lion and the unicorn, and are filled with numerous animals and birds, including dogs, a monkey and a falcon. Comical little rabbits seem to occupy every spare space and beautiful dogs sit looking attentively at the lady.

Candace has used her own dog (a spotted lurcher) and a spotted Old English rabbit, a falcon, a squirrel, a monkey and a pheasant to feature in her rug. The flowers in the background are rare wild ones and for those who would like to try to identify them, they are: cheddar pink, sticky catchfly, rock cinquefoil, saxifrage, diapensia, Alpine snowthistle, wild gladiolus, snowdon lily, fen violet, Teesdale violet, Alpine gentian and red helleborine. Three squares of the rug have been charted as individual cushion designs.

The entire rug is available in kit form from Ehrman (see page 116). To work such a large project requires a real commitment for all but the most dedicated of stitchers and, one suspects, many a rug will become a wall hanging as it seems almost sacrilegious to put such a beautiful article on the floor.

Another idea would be to place the carpet on a table for one and all to admire. Formal dining rooms are often the least-used room in any home and to cover the table, when it is not in use, would be reverting to the medieval custom of having table carpets. At that time, carpets were either rare imported ones, or those embroidered on fine canvas by professional embroiderers or by the ladies of the house. Their purpose was to cover up the rather basic furniture and to impart much needed colour to the bare rooms.

COLOURWAYS
FOR RABBIT

Ap327 (Pa510)	a	
Ap157 (Pa532)	b	
Ap643 (PaD522)	c	
Ap642 (PaD546)	d	
Ap694 (Pa733)	e	
Ap124 (Pa483)	f	
Ap225 (PaD211)	g	
Ap853 (Pa511)	h	
Ap912 (Pa441)	i	
Ap762 (Pa442)	j	
Ap984 (Pa454)	k	
Ap993 (Pa220)	l	

Ap = Appleton (tapestry)
Pa = Paterna (Persian)

YARN AMOUNTS

a	121m	(132yd)
b	52m	(57yd)
c	44m	(48yd)
d	16m	(18yd)
e	11m	(12yd)
f	3m	(4yd)
g	6m	(7yd)
h	10m	(11yd)
i	19m	(21yd)
j	62m	(67yd)
k	23m	(25yd)
l	2m	(3yd)

RABBIT (FROM HUNTING RUG)
LURCHER (FROM HUNTING RUG)
by Candace Bahouth

MATERIALS

Tapestry wool (see Colourways). The amounts given are for tapestry wool worked in basketweave or continental tent stitch. If the design is worked in half-cross stitch, 30 per cent less wool is required. Four strands of Persian wool can be substituted for the double strand of tapestry wool used for this design. (To calculate amounts for Persian wool see page 109.)

7-mesh rug canvas 50cm (20in) square
Tapestry needle
50cm (20in) furnishing fabric for backing
1.8m (6ft) narrow piping cord
Cushion pad (pillow form) 40cm (16in) square
30cm (12in) zip fastener (optional)
Scroll or stretcher frame (optional)
Tools and materials for preparing canvas (see page 111) and for blocking (page 112)

The finished cushion measures 40cm (15½in) square.

COLOURWAYS
FOR LURCHER

Ap327	(Pa510)	a
Ap157	(Pa532)	b
Ap643	(PaD522)	c
Ap642	(PaD546)	d
Ap694	(Pa733)	e
Ap124	(Pa483)	f
Ap225	(PaD211)	g
Ap853	(Pa511)	h
Ap912	(Pa441)	i
Ap762	(Pa442)	j
Ap984	(Pa454)	k
Ap993	(Pa220)	l
Ap207	(Pa870)	m

Ap = Appleton (tapestry)
Pa = Paterna (Persian)

YARN AMOUNTS

a	126m	(137yd)
b	38m	(41yd)
c	36m	(39yd)
d	19m	(21yd)
e	6m	(7yd)
f	2m	(3yd)
g	8m	(9yd)
h	5m	(6yd)
i	11m	(12yd)
j	85m	(93yd)
k	29m	(31yd)
l	2m	(3yd)
m	3m	(4yd)

WORKING THE EMBROIDERY

Prepare the canvas and mount it on the frame, if used (see page 111). Following the chart for the rabbit (opposite page) or the lurcher (above) and using 2 strands of tapestry wool, work the chosen design in basketweave or continental tent stitch, or in half-cross stitch.

BLOCKING AND MAKING UP

Block the completed work (see page 112) and allow it to dry thoroughly. Trim the canvas edges, leaving margins of 2cm (¾in).

From the backing fabric cut a piece 44cm (17in) square. Or, if inserting a zip, cut two pieces as specified on page 114.

From the remaining fabric, cut and join bias strips to cover the piping cord (see page 114). Make up the piping.

If using a zip, insert it in the back cover (see page 114).

Attach the piping to the back cover as described on page 115.

Join the front and back covers as described on page 115, and insert the cushion pad.

SQUIRREL (FROM HUNTING RUG)
by Candace Bahouth

MATERIALS
Tapestry wool (see Colourways). The amounts given are for tapestry wool worked in basketweave or continental tent stitch. If the design is worked in half-cross stitch, 30 per cent less wool is required. Four strands of Persian wool can be substituted for the double strand of tapestry wool used for this design. (To calculate amounts for Persian wool see page 109.)

7-mesh rug canvas 50cm (20in) square
Tapestry needle
50cm (20in) furnishing fabric for backing
1.8m (6ft) narrow piping cord
Cushion pad (pillow form) 40cm (16in) square
30cm (12in) zip fastener (optional)
Scroll or stretcher frame (optional)
Tools and materials for preparing canvas (see page 111) and for blocking (page 112)

HUNTING RUG
by Candace Bahouth

Being worked on large mesh rug canvas the Squirrel (above), Rabbit and Lurcher cushions taken from the Hunting Rug (left) are quite quick to work.

COLOURWAYS
FOR SQUIRREL

Ap327	(Pa510)	a
Ap157	(Pa532)	b
Ap643	(PaD522)	c
Ap642	(PaD546)	d
Ap694	(Pa733)	e
Ap124	(Pa483)	f
Ap225	(PaD211)	g
Ap853	(Pa511)	h
Ap912	(Pa441)	i
Ap762	(Pa442)	j
Ap984	(Pa454)	k
Ap993	(Pa220)	l
Ap207	(Pa870)	m

Ap = Appleton (tapestry)
Pa = Paterna (Persian)

YARN AMOUNTS

a	104m	(114yd)
b	53m	(58yd)
c	50m	(54yd)
d	8m	(9yd)
e	3m	(4yd)
f	23m	(25yd)
g	5m	(6yd)
h	12m	(14yd)
i	15m	(17yd)
j	9m	(10yd)
k	15m	(17yd)
l	8m	(9yd)
m	65m	(71yd)

The finished cushion measures 40cm (15½in) square.

WORKING THE EMBROIDERY

Prepare the canvas and mount it on the frame, if used (see page 111). Following the chart above and using 2 strands of tapestry wool, work the design in basketweave or continental tent stitch, or in half-cross stitch.

BLOCKING AND MAKING UP

Block the completed work (see page 112) and allow it to dry thoroughly. Trim the canvas edges, leaving margins of 2cm (¾in).

From the backing fabric cut a piece 44cm (17in) square. Or, if inserting a zip, cut two pieces as specified on page 114.

From the remaining fabric, cut and join bias strips to cover the piping cord (see page 114). Make up the piping.

If using a zip, insert it in the back cover (see page 114). Attach the piping to the back cover as described on page 115.

Join the front and back covers as described on page 115, and insert the cushion pad.

MEDIEVAL FANTASY
by Margaret Murton

The unicorn, falcon and hare (right) were often used in medieval tapestry, and these animals here form a naïve and somewhat humorous trio — which the designer's husband has dubbed 'the good, the bad and the ugly'. Margaret Murton herself prefers to think of her hare as being comical, not ugly.

Rather than setting the animals in a medieval context, Margaret Murton has turned to Elizabethan embroidery, in which animals, trees and flowers were traced or copied from early books with little regard for their relative scale.

The faded, almost ghostly colours used for the design are reminiscent of those found in the faded needlework chair covers in stately homes, in which the patterns have become mere washes of colour between bold outlines. On close examination the original bright colours can often be detected, but the subtle faded versions have a happy way of accommodating themselves unobtrusively in the colour scheme of any room.

ELIZABETHAN EMBROIDERY

The Elizabethan and Stuart periods of British history have left a rich legacy of embroidery. A glance at the portraits of the day shows how the nobility loved to dress up in lavishly embroidered and bejewelled costumes. Sumptuous court dress, encrusted with flowers and scrolling patterns in metal and silk threads, would have been professionally embroidered. At the same time, the more mundane articles of clothing and household furnishings were made and embroidered by amateurs at home.

Embroidery was a highly fashionable pastime, indeed an essential accomplishment for the women at the Court of Queen Elizabeth I. Printed furnishing fabrics were unknown so colour and decoration for the sparsely furnished Elizabethan houses and castles had to be provided by woven tapestries and embroideries.

Imitation tapestries could be embroidered on linen by the ladies of a house and their servants at a far lower cost than ordering woven ones from France or Flanders. Bed hangings and valances, table carpets and cushions to soften the benches and wooden chairs were also embroidered, along with small pictures (worked for their amusement), often depicting Old Testament stories and based on engravings. The work was generally done in fine tent and/or cross stitch.

Although less costly than tapestry, canvas embroidery was carried out only in the great houses, since materials, both scarce and expensive, had to be ordered from London or the Continent.

Some families retained an embroiderer to draw out designs, other households would rely on the professional embroiderers who travelled from place to place copying out designs in ink on fine linen, or on the governess who might trace designs for her pupil. That so much embroidery has survived from this period is due to the fact it was always considered precious and thus treated with respect. Many pieces have remained in the houses where they were made; others have been moved to other family houses or acquired by museums.

Textile historians have traced the design sources of these embroideries to woodblock prints and engravings in the illustrated Bibles and other books, such as herbals and bestiaries, that proliferated during the sixteenth and seventeenth centuries. *A Book of Beasts, Birds, Flowers, Fruicts, Flies and Wormes*, published by Thomas Johnson in London, 1630, was particularly popular.

The composite arrangements of birds and animals jumbled together and embroidered with scant regard to their true scale may strike us as being somewhat bizarre, until we realize the bird and butterfly stitched to the same size, if not larger, than the neighbouring horse and rhinoceros, have been slavishly copied from their individual representations in early books of natural history. In each case the same sources of design – biblical scenes, flowers, plants and animals – were

RICHARD SACKVILLE, 3RD EARL OF DORSET
by William Larkin

This wonderful picture (right) *of Richard Sackville (painted c. 1613) hangs, with that of his brother, in the Ranger's House, Blackheath, London. A pair of extreme dandies, they vie to outshine each other in the opulent splendour of their attire. It illustrates the extent to which detailed and painstaking decorative embroidery on clothes was taken. It was quite common for Elizabethan courtiers to spend the modern equivalent of £50,000 on a set of clothes which were worn to show off both the quality of materials used and the skill of the elaborate embroidery. They were the most visible status symbols of the period and allowed full scope to the uninhibited and wealthy male to enjoy dressing-up!*

ANIMAL SLIP
from Traquair House

This incongruous mixture of a leopard and a strawberry plant, with a bird in the leaves (right), is a detail from a large panel of canvas-embroidered 'slips', c. 1610, found at Traquair House, the Scottish Borders home of Mr Peter Maxwell Stuart. Never having been used, these slips have remained as bright as the day they were made. (Photograph by Martin Gostelow.)

was borrowed from horticulture – the slips, or cuttings, taken by gardeners for propagation – reflecting the fact that floral motifs generally predominated in this kind of work.

The brilliantly coloured panels of small-scale plants, flowers, birds and animals dating from 1610 at Traquair House, in the Scottish Border country, are superb examples of this form of needlework. Intended as slips and borders, they were never used but put in storage, and so remain as bright as the day they were embroidered. Still uncut from the canvas, they provide an insight into how this form of appliqué was worked.

Each panel, measuring about 76 by 56 centimetres (30 by 22 inches), contains a great many designs – one has seventy-two different flower plants arranged in neat rows. The designs, drawn in ink, then outlined in black silk, are placed very close together so as not to waste any of the linen background, which is far finer than the canvas normally used for embroidery today.

used time and time again with only slight variation. Animals (not quite so popular as flowers) appear in the most unlikely places, particularly at the sides and corners of the decorative borders of allegorical pictures, often adding a humorous touch to an otherwise solemn subject. They are also to be found on embroidered carpets; a stag under a tree is pictured in one of the three medallions of the Gifford Table Carpet, and a variety of animals, including sheep and hunting dogs, help to enliven the borders of the Bradford Table Carpet. Both of these sixteenth-century carpets are now in the Victoria and Albert Museum, in London.

Small-scale designs were worked as 'slips' and used as appliqué motifs on velvet and wool curtains, valances and bed hangings. The term 'slip'

DOVES AND FRUIT
by Margaret Murton

The Elizabethan-style embroidery (right) captures the magical mood of a perfect English summer's day with just the right quantity of sunlight to catch the whiter than white wings of the fantail doves and to throw purple shadows on their feathers. The charming border intertwined with scrolling stems is strongly influenced by Elizabethan needlework, in which flowers, leaves and small animals were interspersed with regular patterns of strapwork or scrolls.

The designer Margaret Murton, a musician, watercolourist and country-lover, has always been drawn to the Elizabethan era by the romantic melancholy of its music, its poetry and its delight in the minutiae of nature, as expressed in embroidery.

Some time ago, when searching for ideas for an arbour for her own garden, she visited Compton Wynyates, in Warwickshire. The dovecote of this manor house provided the inspiration for this charming Elizabethan-style hanging.

The linen was almost certainly stretched on a frame and the embroidery worked by several people. Once the whole panel was completed, the individual motifs would have been cut out and stiffened on the back with a flour paste to arrest fraying, before being stitched down on wool or velvet. When the background wore out, the slips could be transferred to new cloth.

One of the Traquair panels shows a delightful *mélange* of exotic birds and animals placed among the most unlikely fruit and vegetable plants. In each case the plant is drawn to resemble a tree, with an animal at the base and a bird in the boughs. Both flora and fauna are juxtaposed and depicted with a fine disregard for realism. Thus, for example, a spotted leopard stands underneath a strawberry plant, which has red strawberries but blue and white flowers, with a bird, possibly a jay, on the stem. A wild boar prowls beneath a tree bearing marrows (squash); another panel depicts a unicorn below a grapevine – the grapes being

larger than the animal. One wonders who had the imagination to think up these strange combinations which include a griffin, dragon, crocodile and turkey, each placed beneath an identically shaped plant.

Animals also figure prominently in the canvaswork slips applied to the famous Oxburgh Hangings. These were worked by Mary Queen of Scots and Bess of Hardwick, Countess of Shrewsbury, who served as Mary's companion and jailer during the Queen's nineteen-year imprisonment in England. Originally intended as wall hangings, these green velvet panels were later converted to bed curtains (now in Oxburgh Hall, in Norfolk) and one was cut up to make a valance (now in the Victoria and Albert Museum). The medallions worked by Mary reflect the sixteenth-century fascination with emblems, a type of cartoon in which objects were used to illustrate puns on Latin words and texts. Thus, the seemingly innocent selection of creatures she chose to em-

MARY QUEEN OF SCOTS EMBLEMS

Slips (right) *embroidered by Mary Queen of Scots in silks on linen canvas, c. 1570, applied to velvet hangings, now at Oxburgh Hall, Norfolk, on loan from the Victoria and Albert Museum, London. Many of these embroidered emblems illustrated puns on Latin words and texts and so have a symbolic meaning. The two slips shown here are 'A Crocodil' and 'A Byrd of America'.*

EMBLEMS
by Mary Queen of Scots

These slips (left), *like those on the opposite page, are on display at Oxburgh Hall, Norfolk, England.*

broider had, in many cases, a symbolic meaning. The easiest to understand is the 'delphin' (dolphin), a pun on the word 'dauphin'; she had married the Dauphin of France in 1558. On another slip, the lion, king of beasts, stands on a squared floor, which may represent a cage – a possible reference to her own imprisonment. But what does one make of the 'knotted serpentes'? The Scottish historian Margaret Swain, in her book *The Needlework of Mary Queen of Scots* (1973), interprets the meaning of some of the emblems and reproduces the engravings from which many of the animals were copied.

MYTHOLOGICAL BEASTS

Other examples of embroidery worked by Mary Queen of Scots and Bess of Hardwick, both individually and together, can be seen at Hardwick Hall, in Derbyshire. This magnificent house, which has remained virtually unaltered since it was built by Bess (when widowed) in the late sixteenth century, contains marvellous tapestries, embroideries and furniture, including an amazing 'sea-dog' table. The legs of this heavy walnut table represent mythological creatures with dogs' heads, women's breasts, wings and dolphins' tails. Incongruously, they rest on four tortoises – a pun on the saying 'Make haste slowly'.

Animals form part of many heraldic devices, and coats of arms were often carved in stone, or moulded in plasterwork friezes for vast Elizabethan mansions. At Hardwick, for example, Bess's own coat of arms, featuring two stags, is placed above the fireplace in both the entrance hall and the drawing room. The royal coat of arms, with the familiar lion and unicorn, is incorporated in the painted plasterwork frieze of the Great High Chamber. This frieze depicts mythological tales, including a representation of the huntress Diana with her maidens, surrounded by beasts, and is above a set of eight Brussels tapestries.

CREWELWORK HANGING OF LEAVES AND BEASTS

An English crewelwork hanging (right) *with exotic leaves sprouting from twisting stems, growing out of hillocks, with birds and beasts hidden among the greenery. This type of hanging, made for a four-poster bed, was popular from the late seventeenth century onwards.*

The griffin (bottom left) *and a squirrel* (centre left) *were copied by Judith Gussin for cushion designs.*

The hanging, dating from the early eighteenth century, is in the Collection of the Embroiderers' Guild at Hampton Court Palace. (Photograph by Dudley Moss.)

GRIFFIN AND SQUIRREL
by Judith Gussin

These cushions (opposite page) *designed by Judith Gussin show the influence of seventeenth-century needlework.*

SEVENTEENTH-CENTURY NEEDLEWORK

The main source of designs for most amateur embroidery was still the engraving published in books. One particular lion and leopard, shown seated and facing each other, keep cropping up in the embroidery of the time, and were evidently copied from one of these engravings. One young girl, Hannah Smith, used them most boldly on a casket she finished in 1654 when she was not quite twelve years old. It is in the Whitworth Art Gallery, Manchester (see page 28).

Needlework was an important part of the education of a young girl of noble birth. She would have started her embroidery with a sampler (a word derived from the Latin *exemplum*, or French *essamplaire*, meaning 'example'), which employed a variety of embroidery and needlelace stitches and patterns; this would later serve as a useful reference when designing. She would then progress to small pictures, using raised work.

This form of embroidery, now called stumpwork, had raised or padded figures. It was used to make embroidered pictures and also to decorate such objects as mirror frames and caskets. These items are believed to be among the earliest forms of embroidery kits. The biblical scenes on the main panels were drawn or printed on silk and, it is thought, sold by print- and booksellers in the City of London. Once the embroidery was completed, it would be returned to the print-seller to be made up into the finished article.

A particularly popular form of embroidery was crewelwork, in which swirling floral motifs were worked in wool yarns on linen or cotton twill. A great variety of surface stitches were used for this work (which is sometimes called Jacobean embroidery, after the period in which it became fashionable, during the reign of James I), and the effect was often extremely elaborate.

continued on page 28

GRIFFIN
by Judith Gussin

MATERIALS

Tapestry wool (see Colourways). The amounts given are for tapestry wool worked in basketweave or continental tent stitch. If the design is worked in half-cross stitch, 30 per cent less wool is required. Double-thread or interlock canvas is suitable for all three types of tent stitch, but if basketweave or continental tent is used an ordinary mono canvas may be substituted. Two strands of Persian wool or three strands of crewel can be substituted for the single strand of tapestry wool used for this design. (To calculate amounts for crewel or Persian wool see page 109.)

12-mesh double or mono interlock canvas 50cm (20in) square

Size 18 tapestry needle

50cm (20in) furnishing fabric for backing

1.8m (6ft) narrow piping cord

Cushion pad (pillow form) 40cm (16in) square

30cm (12in) zip fastener (optional)

Scroll or stretcher frame (optional)

Tools and materials for preparing canvas (see page 111) and for blocking (page 112)

The finished cushion measures 38×39cm (15×15½in).

COLOURWAYS FOR GRIFFIN

An3034	(Pa510)	a
An0506	(PaD546)	b
An0860	(Pa603)	c
An0388	(Pa444)	d
An3276	(Pa445)	e
An0729	(Pa755)	f ☐
An0987	(Pa420)	g
An0392	(Pa463)	h
An0391	(Pa464)	i
An0503	(PaD211)	j
An069	(Pa922)	k
An0161	(Pa503)	l

An = Anchor (tapisserie)
Pa = Paterna (Persian)

YARN AMOUNTS

a	87m	(95yd)
b	64m	(70yd)
c	65m	(71yd)
d	16m	(18yd)
e	34m	(38yd)
f	5m	(6yd)
g	22m	(24yd)
h	12m	(13yd)
i	21m	(23yd)
j	9m	(10yd)
k	21m	(23yd)
l	12m	(13yd)

WORKING THE EMBROIDERY

Prepare the canvas and mount it on the frame, if used (see page 111). Following the chart on the right and using a single strand of tapestry wool, work the design in basketweave or continental tent stitch, or in half-cross stitch.

BLOCKING AND MAKING UP

Block the completed work (see page 112) and allow it to dry thoroughly. Trim the canvas edges, leaving margins of 2cm (¾in).

From the backing fabric cut a piece 42×43cm (16½×17in). Or, if inserting a zip, cut two pieces as specified on page 114.

From the remaining fabric, cut and join bias strips to cover the piping cord (see page 114). Make up the piping.

If using a zip, insert it in the back cover (see page 114).

Attach the piping to the back cover as described on page 115.

Join the front and back covers as described on page 115, and insert the cushion pad.

GRIFFIN CUSHION
by Judith Gussin

The Griffin cushion design captures the mood of an early crewelwork hanging, belonging to the Embroiderers' Guild, at Hampton Court Palace outside London, which was made as a curtain for a four-poster bed. It is a glorious mixture of exotic leaves sprouting incongruously from twisting stems growing out of hillocks, with birds and animals.

The griffin and a lion sit either side of the 'trees' with two rabbits at the base. Hidden amongst the foliage is a phoenix, a cockatrice and an Oriental pheasant.

The animals have been copied from the Stent and Overton pattern books, used for so many Elizabethan embroidery designs, and the griffin from a later edition called A new Booke of all Sortes of Beasties *– or a pleasant way to teach yeong children to read.*

The Squirrel and Griffin cushion designs (previous page) complement one another and in both cases the animals are surrounded by a great variety of exotic leaves. The squirrel with his acorn looks very appealing, while the griffin, a mythological creature that is half-cat and half-eagle, makes rather more impact with its feathered wings and menacing face.

Judith Gussin's arrangement of leaves around the animals give the cushions a sense of the 'Jacobean' hanging although it would be difficult, on canvas, to achieve the same textured effect as the original which contains a great variety of stitches — long and short, stem, split, brick, chain, flat, bullion and French knots, Cretan, wheatear, detached chain, and laid fillings, a palette which makes our own repertoire of common canvas stitches seem very paltry.

This tradition, along with most of the English styles of needlework, was taken to the New World by the colonists, beginning in the early seventeenth century. There, despite shortages of materials, the making of beautiful and useful textiles soon became an important part of domestic life, just as it had been in the Old Country.

ANIMALS IN PAINTING AND SCULPTURE

During the Middle Ages European painting had been largely restricted to religious subjects; and animals, like humans, generally appeared only where the religious content required it. From the Renaissance onwards, however, a new interest in individual humans and in the natural world was apparent in both painting and sculptures. Portraits of important or wealthy people were painted, and in these portraits the occasional animal appeared. One especially endearing example is the little dog, slightly resembling a Yorkshire terrier, in the foreground of Van Eyck's painting of the betrothal of the Arnolfini, in the National Gallery, in London.

Considerably less accomplished, but nonetheless charming, is a delightful family portrait with animals painted by an unknown English artist in 1567. This portrait of William Brooke, 10th Lord Cobham, and his family (which hangs in Longleat House, Wiltshire) is a somewhat primitive painting lacking in perspective, and the children's pets add a touch of humour and life. A small dog is jumping up at one of the six children, who sit very solemnly around a table. One child has a bird on his wrist, another is holding a marmoset, and a parrot struts around the middle of the table.

By the middle of the next century, the equestrian portrait had become a well-established genre of European painting. A particularly famous example is the one of Charles I on his horse by Sir Anthony van Dyck, now in London's National Gallery. Another fine Van Dyck portrait of the King, standing in front of his horse, hangs in the Louvre. From this time onwards, portraits of gentlemen and ladies on horseback were to become increasingly popular.

The earliest-known English equestrian statue is the almost life-size 'Lumley Horseman', *c.* 1580, which represents King Edward III in full armour. It was commissioned by Lord Lumley to be placed in a niche in the wall of the Great Hall of Lumley Castle, County Durham, and is carved from wood and painted in oils.

This very solid wood carving is in marked contrast to the immensely fine work that would be done a century later by Grinling Gibbons for buildings such as St Paul's Cathedral, London, and Petworth House, Sussex. One of Gibbons' most remarkable and unusual groups is a limewood carving of duck, partridge and woodcock, and bunches of different fish, hanging from a garland of flowers above a lobster, a crab and other shellfish. This was carved around 1680-95 and is set into the overmantel of the entrance hall at Kirtlington Park, Oxfordshire.

HANNAH SMITH'S CASKET

This superb casket was begun by Hannah Smith in 1654 and, according to a note she left in the box, finished two years later when she was nearly twelve years old. The motif of a lion and leopard, at the top of the casket is taken from A new Booke of all Sortes of Beasties, *and recurs frequently in embroidery of this period. The casket is in the Whitworth Art Gallery, Manchester.*

FOREST FIRE
by Piero Di Cosimo (1462-1521)

The Florentine painter Piero Di Cosimo painted classic fables, frequently including animals and birds in nature or fantastic shapes, such as appear in this painting which was probably executed in the late 1480s. It is one of a series of four panels (two in the Metropolitan Museum, New York, and the others in the Wadsworth Athenaeum, Hartford and the Ottawa National Gallery) illustrating scenes in the life of primitive man. These panels probably formed a frieze in the house of Franceso del Pugliese, described by Vasari.

Piero Di Cosimo's fascination with natural species was typical of the fifteenth century. This picture is unusual, however, in treating animals as the main theme. A deer, a hyena, a bear, a bull and numerous birds are among the many creatures that can be identified in The Forest Fire. *The curious habit of giving quadrupeds human faces was an extension of the medieval notion that certain animals symbolized particular moral behaviour or character traits, and the general relationship between man and animals would not have been missed by the Renaissance viewer.*

THE ELEGANT AND THE EXOTIC

'In this high baroque style, halted at a point on the frontiers of rococo where the extravagant magic of later decades is all implicit, how easily the same aesthetic mood glides from church to palace, from palace to ballroom . . . clouds drift, cherubim are on the wing, and swarms of putti, baptised in flight from the Greek Anthology, break loose over the tombs . . . Chinese pagodas, African palms, Nile Pyramids and then a Mexican volcano and the conifers and wigwams of Red Indians spring up in Arcady. Walls of mirror reflect these scenes.'

A Time of Gifts, Patrick Leigh Fermor

PARAKEET AND PINEAPPLE
by Sue Rangeley

The delicate detail of Sue Rangeley's painting (left) of her Parakeet and Pineapple design is captured perfectly in the finished canvaswork cushion on page 39.

ELEPHANTS AND WARRIORS
by Anita Gunnett

The instructions for Anita Gunnett's stylized Elephants and Warriors cushion (right) are given on page 34.

PINK CAT
by Sarah Windrum

Sarah Windrum's embroidered cat (above) has to be the original 'cat that ate the bowl of cream'; it is quite the most opulent and complacently content cat ever seen. In fact, you can almost hear it purring, very loudly, because it is so pleased with life.

There is also something thoroughly decadent about the lush pink, grey, cream and white colours, and the eclectic assortment of fabrics from different eras which surround the cat as it sits on its plump cushion.

The eighteenth century was an era of great elegance and refinement, of magnificent buildings by Sir Christopher Wren and Robert Adam, with splendid interiors, fine furniture and porcelain. Architects such as William Kent in Britain and Ange-Jacques Gabriel in France created houses and palaces that were closer in spirit to the classical ideal than to the grandiose monuments of the baroque.

Exotic merchandise such as silks, spices, embroideries, porcelain and precious jewels became more readily available from countries along the 'silk route' and this trade led to an exchange of design influences from one culture to another.

Embroidery was no longer needed for curtains and hangings. By the middle of the century there were some 12,000 to 15,000 looms weaving fine silk damasks and brocades in Spitalfields, London, and printed fabrics were being produced in London by the 1760s. Instead, the ladies of the house embroidered canvas for chair seats and backs, firescreens, and beautiful carpets filled with flowers, while quilted silk bedcovers were made in professional workshops.

In England and North America there was a vogue for embroidering dainty pictures in coloured silks on satin, the faces of figures, and sometimes the background, being painted rather than stitched. Romantic pastoral scenes of the gentry dressed as shepherds and shepherdesses, with sheep in the foreground, epitomized the mood of the moment.

A regional variant of the pastoral theme was a series of 'fishing lady' canvaswork pictures produced in the area around Boston, Massachusetts. In these pictures an elegantly dressed lady is shown fishing in a pond, surrounded by flowering and fruit-laden trees and scampering animals.

Oriental influences were to be seen in the many exotic birds, Chinese pheasants in particular, that appeared in needlework and woven textiles.

continued on page 36

ELEPHANTS AND WARRIORS
by Anita Gunnett

MATERIALS

Tapestry wool (see Colourways). The amounts given are for tapestry wool worked in basketweave or continental tent stitch. If the design is worked in half-cross stitch, 30 per cent less wool is required. Double-thread or interlock canvas is suitable for all three types of tent stitch, but if basketweave or continental tent is used an ordinary mono canvas may be substituted. Two strands of Persian wool or three strands of crewel can be substituted for the single strand of tapestry wool used for this design. (To calculate amounts for crewel or Persian wool see page 109.)

12-mesh double or mono interlock canvas 55cm (22in) square
Size 18 tapestry needle
55cm (21in) furnishing fabric for backing
1.9m (6½ft) narrow piping cord
Cushion pad (pillow form) 45cm (17in) square
30cm (12in) zip fastener (optional)
Scroll or stretcher frame (optional)
Tools and materials for preparing canvas (see page 111) and for blocking (page 112)

The finished cushion measures 43cm (16¾in) square.

WORKING THE EMBROIDERY

Prepare the canvas and mount it on the frame, if used (see page 111). Only the lower two rows of the walking figures are given on the chart. Following the chart opposite and using a single strand of tapestry wool, work the charted part of the design in basketweave or continental tent stitch, or in half-cross stitch.

To complete the top part of the design, follow the chart for the figures, placing them in 54 rows of stitches in the background colour. Place the elephant from the lower left-hand corner of the chart at the right-hand side of the top of the design, so that the lowest front hoof is 3 stitches from the striped strip and the right side of this hoof is 21 stitches from the border on the right. Place the soldier with the bow so that the lowest foot is 3 stitches from the striped strip and the left side of this foot is 16 stitches from the border on the left. Place the goose between the elephant and the soldier. Continue the border up the sides and across the top of the design, working the upper corners as for the lower corners.

BLOCKING AND MAKING UP

Block the completed work (see page 112) and allow it to dry thoroughly. Trim the canvas edges, leaving margins of 2cm (¾in).

From the backing fabric cut a piece 47cm (18¼in) square. Or, if inserting a zip, cut two pieces as specified on page 114.

From the remaining fabric, cut and join bias strips to cover the piping cord (see page 114). Make up the piping.

If using a zip, insert it in the back cover (see page 114).

Attach the piping to the back cover as described on page 115.

Join the front and back covers as described on page 115, and insert the cushion pad.

COLOURWAYS FOR ELEPHANTS AND WARRIORS

An0849 (Pa511) a
An0848 (Pa513) b
An0902 (Pa443) c
An0725 (Pa445) d
An069 (Pa922) e
An0392 (Pa463) f
An0984 (Pa462) g
An0403 (Pa220) h

An = Anchor (tapisserie)
Pa = Paterna (Persian)

YARN AMOUNTS

a	53m	(58yd)
b	65m	(71yd)
c	170m	(186yd)
d	36m	(40yd)
e	15m	(17yd)
f	29m	(32yd)
g	6m	(7yd)
h	2m	(3yd)

ELEPHANTS AND WARRIORS
by Anita Gunnett

The Indian elephants striding across this cushion (left), followed by soldiers, trumpeters and geese, are taken from a late-eighteenth-century embroidered hanging depicting the Battle of Kurukshetra, as described in the Mahabharata, *an epic poem about India's origins. The hanging, which is in the Victoria and Albert Museum in London, has a great many elephants, animals and soldiers in eighteenth-century costume parading about in a gloriously haphazard fashion.*

Anita Gunnett, the needlepoint designer, has selected just four of the characters and shown them in a highly stylized manner, processing in an orderly manner between striped horizontal bands and a formal border.

Elephants have always played an important part in Indian life, being used as mounts for hunting, for pulling heavy loads, for transport and for ceremonial parades. Due to this importance they have figured extensively in carpets, fabrics and embroideries over the centuries, and have been given their own fabulously embroidered cloths and head coverings, which are still made to be worn in parades and on other special occasions.

CHERUB AND LION
by Lucinda Ganderton

The Cherub and Lion wall hanging (right) *is Lucinda Ganderton's own reworking of Roman classical imagery.*

Visits to the Renaissance palazzi *and villas of northern Italy first stimulated her interest in these patterns: she drew and photographed mythical beasts, cornucopias, vines and urns decorating the walls of the Medici and the Gonzagas in the warm tones of Florence and Mantua. Back in England, she saw the same designs recurring around her as integral parts of eighteenth-century London architecture and especially in the neo-classical elegance of Syon House and the exuberant plasterwork of Claydon House in Buckinghamshire.*

The motifs in the hanging are drawn from a wide base of original source material. Within its egg-and-dart border, the typically late-eighteenth-century salmon pink and Wedgwood blue background come from the main staircase at Claydon; the vine leaves, from the Gonzagas' palace; the urn from her own parents' garden. The greyhound, leopard and the musical cherub are taken from Joseph Beunat's definitive catalogue of Empire-style ornaments, Recueil des dessins d'ornements d'architecture, *1813.*

The design is unmistakably of the twentieth century, yet a tribute to its classical antecedents.

Embroidery imported from China also adorned the homes of the wealthy, especially in the early 1700s. A particularly splendid example, some hangings for a state bed, were discovered only recently at Calke Abbey, in Derbyshire, still in their original packing case, the colours glowing like new. Among the motifs worked in silk and gold threads are a variety of birds and animals, including gracefully swooping herons and rapacious lions and dragons.

Towards the end of the century the fashion for neo-classical interiors and for the delicate furniture of Hepplewhite and Sheraton called for plain-coloured fabrics for upholstery and curtains. For this reason canvaswork, for the first time in several centuries, ceased to be popular.

It is difficult to imagine decorating a house without printed fabrics, but apart from the highly expensive imports these were not really available until the middle of the eighteenth century.

THE INDIAN CONNECTION

The first printed fabrics to reach Europe had come from India, where the great wealth of intricate patterns and superior knowledge of weaving and dyeing techniques had combined to make it one of the world's greatest textile producing countries. The first travellers had sent back word of the luxuriously embroidered costumes of the Mughal Court.

The superiority of Indian textile printing and painting techniques, and the knowledge of resist-dyeing using different mordants to achieve several colours from one dye, had existed since medieval times and probably earlier. There was, consequently, a great demand for Indian printed fabrics in Europe and Persia in the seventeenth and eighteenth centuries, and even earlier from Japan and southeast Asia.

The original cotton hangings imported to England by the East India Company in the early 1600s were considered too 'foreign' in style to find popularity. The palampores (hangings) with bright red flowers would have seemed garish beside the English crewelwork curtains embroidered in blues and greens. So English hangings, featuring large branching stems incorporating flowers and small animals, were sent to India as examples of the type of work that would be more acceptable.

Instead of simply copying these designs, the Indians changed the trees (so they would appeal to their Mughal customers as well as to the Europeans), to look more like those found in Persian-Mughal art, which had, in turn, been influenced by the asymmetrical lines of Chinese paintings.

The resulting painted Indian 'Tree of Life' cotton hangings, or 'chintz', with large twisting branches rising out of pyramid-shaped mounds, with exotic leaves, fruit and birds, were a great success. Embroidered versions followed, then lengths of cloth embroidered in fine chain stitch with scrolling patterns of leaves and flowers to be used for curtains and bed hangings.

To protect English weavers, the importation of Indian chintz was forbidden from 1721 until the early nineteenth century but the designs were copied, in England and in France, and versions of the Indian 'Tree of Life' have remained in fashion in one form or another ever since.

By the end of the eighteenth century, the British fabric-printing industry was well established. Originally centred in London, it gradually moved to Manchester. A machine capable of rotary-printing up to sixteen colours in a single design was patented in 1783; in the early 1800s it was used, for example, to print fabric with designs based on Audubon's *Birds of America* (published in four volumes between 1827 and 1838).

THE ROCOCO MENAGERIE

The prevailing style in the decorative arts in the first half of the century – rococo – drew its original inspiration from the natural world, transforming the gently curved shapes of shells, flowers and other vegetation into a profusion of exuberantly swirling S-curves. Animals and bird forms also sometimes appeared, especially in the English form of rococo, which owed much of its character to Chinese art.

Some superb examples of English rococo can be seen at Claydon House, in Buckinghamshire, which is typical of the splendid eighteenth-century houses built by the powerful Whig landowners as they vyed to outshine one another. The moment the politically ambitious 2nd Lord Verney inherited Claydon in 1752, he set about enlarging it on a grand scale to try to outdo his neighbour and political opponent, Lord Grenville, whose own estate, Stowe, had employed the talents of such architects as Sir John Vanbrugh and William Kent, as well as the landscape gardener 'Capability' Brown. Lord Verney added an enormous ballroom and rotunda to Claydon House and a suite of rococo rooms adorned with extravagant

HO-HO BIRD
from Claydon House

The sculpted ho-ho bird (below) *forms part of the exotic rococo decoration at Claydon House, Buckinghamshire, designed and made by Luke Lightfoot for the Earl of Verney around 1769. A pair of the birds sit above a door that once led from the hall to the rotunda and ballroom. Claydon House belongs to the National Trust.*

TUREEN AND CENTREPIECE
from the Northumberland Service

A tureen (right), *with a pheasant forming the handle of the lid, and a centrepiece* (below) *are among 120 surviving pieces of the Meissen porcelain 'Northumberland Service' of 1745.*

The 'Northumberland Service', owned by the Duke of Northumberland, is on display at Alnwick Castle, Northumberland.

PARAKEET AND PINEAPPLE
by Sue Rangeley

This tent stitch embroidery (opposite page) *is worked in thirteen soft tones.*

carvings by Luke Lightfoot. This included a 'Chinese Room' decorated in the highly fashionable chinoiserie style, with panels and overmantels decorated with flowers, fruit, birds, beasts, swags and wreaths.

In striving to complete this fanciful showplace the Earl bankrupted himself, and his relatives were later forced to demolish two-thirds of the house in order to pay for the upkeep of the remainder. It now belongs to the National Trust.

The exuberance of the rococo style can also be seen in the delightful embroidered hanging (see page 36) designed by Lucinda Ganderton, who drew inspiration from Claydon House, as well as from the more classical interior of Syon House, Middlesex. This was the work of Robert Adam, done in the 1760s for the Duke of Northumberland. Among the Duke's possessions was a magnificent dinner service, decorated mainly with animals, made by Meissen around 1745 and originally presented as a gift to the British Envoy in Dresden. Each of the surviving 120 pieces of the Northumberland Service (now on display at Alnwick Castle, in Northumberland) is decorated with different animals. The painted images are copied from a variety of old engravings and surrounded by a garland of botanically correct

flowers, drawn to a much larger scale than the animals. This incongruous mixture is not dissimilar to the arrangement of animals and flowers used in earlier needlework pictures.

Many of the handles of the dishes are modelled to represent animals; a particularly charming example is a pheasant that perches on the lid of a large tureen.

Another Meissen service owned by the Duke of Northumberland, and also displayed at Alnwick Castle, has scenes from the *Fables* of La Fontaine. It was made a little later, in 1772-6, in a far more classical style, with rams' heads used as handles on the tureen, and the animal scenes placed in the centre of the dishes, with a green and gold border around the edge.

Tureens in the shape of animals were being made by the Chelsea factory, in London, around the middle of the eighteenth century. Among them are a whole boar's head and a life-size hen with one chick on her back and another under her wing. The same factory also produced shallow sauceboats in the form of plaice – with the fish lying flat and their tails being the handles.

continued on page 42

COLOURWAYS FOR PARAKEET AND PINEAPPLE

Ap964	(Pa201)	a	
Ap963	(Pa202)	b	
Ap962	(Pa203)	c	
Ap961	(Pa204)	d	
Ap223	(PaD234)	e	
Ap221	(Pa924)	f	
Ap708	(Pa874)	g	
Ap974	(Pa461)	h	
Ap973	(Pa462)	i	
Ap313	(Pa750)	j	
Ap996	(Pa773)	k	
Ap872	(Pa755)	l	
Ap695	(Pa732)	m	

Ap = Appleton (tapestry)
Pa = Paterna (Persian)

YARN AMOUNTS

a	66m	(72yd)
b	10m	(11yd)
c	49m	(54yd)
d	3m	(3yd)
e	9m	(10yd)
f	88m	(96yd)
g	18m	(20yd)
h	73m	(79yd)
i	9m	(10yd)
j	25m	(27yd)
k	17m	(19yd)
l	15m	(16yd)
m	12m	(13yd)

PARAKEET AND PINEAPPLE
by Sue Rangeley

MATERIALS

Tapestry wool (see Colourways). The amounts given are for tapestry wool worked in basketweave or continental tent stitch. If the design is worked in half-cross stitch, 30 per cent less wool is required. Double-thread or interlock canvas is suitable for all three types of tent stitch, but if basketweave or continental tent is used an ordinary mono canvas may be substituted. Three strands of Persian wool or four strands of crewel can be substituted for the single strand of tapestry wool used for this design. (To calculate amounts for crewel or Persian wool see page 109.)

10-mesh double or mono interlock canvas 55cm (22in) square
Size 18 tapestry needle
55cm (22in) furnishing fabric for backing
1.9m (6½ft) narrow piping cord, or furnishing fringe
Cushion pad (pillow form) 48cm (18in) square
35cm (14in) zip fastener (optional)
Scroll or stretcher frame (optional)
Tools and materials for preparing canvas (see page 111) and for blocking (page 112)

The finished cushion measures 46cm (18in) square.

WORKING THE EMBROIDERY

Prepare the canvas and mount it on the frame, if used (see page 111). Following the chart on the right and using a single strand of tapestry wool, work the design in basketweave or continental tent stitch, or in half-cross stitch.

BLOCKING AND MAKING UP

Block the completed work (see page 112) and allow it to dry thoroughly. Trim the canvas edges, leaving margins of 2cm (¾in).

From the backing fabric cut a piece 50cm (19½in) square. Or, if inserting a zip, cut two pieces as specified on page 114.

If piping the edge, cut and join bias strips of fabric to cover the piping cord (see page 114). Make up the piping.

If using a zip, insert it in the back cover (see page 114).

Attach the piping to the back cover as described on page 115. Alternatively, stitch furnishing fringe around the edge, with the fringe lying towards the centre.

Join the front and back covers as described on page 115, and insert the cushion pad.

PARAKEET AND PINEAPPLE
by Sue Rangeley

The highly stylized group of a parakeet, pineapple and peaches on this embroidered canvaswork cushion was inspired by old prints and has been arranged in a manner that echoes the formal Dutch still life oil paintings of the seventeenth and eighteenth centuries.

Sue Rangeley, the designer, is one of Britain's leading embroidery artists. Her exquisite, detailed embroideries, in cotton, silk, and metal threads, are worked on hand-painted fabrics which are often quilted. She works to private commission, designing and making evening and wedding clothes, jackets, evening bags, and large-scale quilts, cushions, carpets and screens for interiors.

The Parakeet and Pineapple cushion followed on from a commission for a needlepoint carpet with a coordinated series of cushions, featuring birds and fruit placed within a formal border of leaves. The border of this cushion has a delicate feather motif, and the colours are soft tones of grey mixed with flecks of pale yellow to echo the decorative pattern of the bird's feathers and the changing tints of colour in the foliage and fruit.

This needlepoint would make a lovely picture. There must be hundreds of embroidery designs, intended as cushions, that have ended up in a frame hanging in pride of place on the wall. The maker cannot bear the idea of the finished work being subjected to the wear and tear of everyday life, particularly if it is their first effort.

SPORTING ART

Among the first British printed fabrics, produced in London in the 1760s, were shooting and fishing scenes, with elegantly clad sportsmen standing near classical ruins – thus combining two of the foremost interests of the cultivated country gentlemen of the day. This was a great era for sporting art. The English passion for field sports and racing ensured that sooner or later the animals involved in these sports would be included in landscape paintings and portraits.

In the late seventeenth century it had been fashionable for landowners to be painted participating in one of their sports, generally hunting, with their country house portrayed in the background. This gave way to straightforward pictures of racing, shooting and hunting. James Seymour's racing scene 'A Race Over the Long Course at Newmarket' was painted around 1731. A few years later, in 1740, John Wootton, the first English artist to specialize in sporting pictures, painted 'The Shooting Party' which shows Frederick, Prince of Wales (son of George II), and two companions, surrounded by spaniels and dead pheasants.

The great subscription hunts, such as the Heythrope, Wrekin and Pychley, were founded in the middle of the eighteenth century; previous-ly, hunts had been run privately by the major landowners. To give courage in the hunting field, it was traditional for a parting drink, or stirrup cup, to be taken at the meet of the foxhounds; silver stirrup cups in the shape of fox heads were introduced for this custom around 1770. The earliest of these were made by Thomas Pitts of Piccadilly, London, and were engraved with the traditional toast 'Success to Fox Hunting and Friends Round the Wrekin'.

By the 1760s George Stubbs – today acknowledged as the master painter of horses – had begun to make his name as an animal artist. The 3rd Duke of Richmond commissioned a painting of himself with the 'Charlton Hunt', and another of his 'Racehorses at Exercise'. Stubbs painted these while staying at the Duke's country estate, Goodwood House, in Sussex, where the pictures may be seen.

Two years later, Stubbs painted a remarkably vivid hunting scene, entitled 'The Grosvenor Hunt'. Here hounds splash excitedly in the river, where they have a stag at bay, while Lord Grosvenor, his friends and hunt servants observe the action on horseback.

Stubbs was also painting horse portraits for the 2nd Marquess of Rockingham, an enthusiastic racegoer and breeder of race horses. The superb groups of 'Mares and Foals' are now world

WATER SPANIEL
by George Stubbs

A water spaniel (right) *painted by George Stubbs for the Earl of Yarborough, Master of the Brocklesby Hounds, in 1804. This breed of delightfully shaggy-looking spaniel is now extinct, but at the time was a popular shooting dog. One of the artist's last works, this picture was painted for a man who had been his patron for over thirty years. It is owned by the present Earl of Yarborough, of Brocklesby Park.*

TIGERS
by Sue Rangeley

At first glance the three tigers stalking through the jungle in this embroidered picture (right) *are hard to discern, as they almost merge into the foliage, whose subtle shades of brown, beige, cream, pink and blue were derived from faded Indian miniatures.*

The Indian collection in London's Victoria and Albert Museum and the Indian miniatures in the British Museum provided Sue Rangeley with ideas for the group of tigers. Although the design, with its formal border, is intended as a picture, it could be used as a long cushion, finished perhaps with decorative tassels and braids.

TWO ELEPHANTS
by the Royal School of
Needlework

*Designed by Marion Beatty
when she was working at the
Royal School of Needlework the
'Two Elephants' (right) have a
distinctly Indian flavour. The
oversize, bold outlines of leaves
and flowers are reminiscent of
Indian chintz fabric patterns
and the soft mulberry, biscuit
and strawberry tones evoke the
hot dusty colours of that
continent.*

*Indian cotton chintz fabrics
for decorating were already
firmly established in England by
the eighteenth century. Samuel
Pepys records in his diary on 5th
September, 1663 that he bought
his wife 'a chinte. . . . that is
paynted Indian callico for to line
her new study which is very
pretty'.*

*The elephants of India and
the East had been legendary in
Europe since Marco Polo's
reports in the thirteenth century.
Describing Kublai Khan's new
year celebrations he says, 'I can
also assure you for a fact that on
this day the great Khan receives
gifts of more than 100,000
white horses of great beauty and
price. And on this day also there
is a procession of his elephants,
fully 5,000 in number, all
draped in fine cloths embroidered
with beasts and birds.' These
exotic images captured the
imagination of European artists
and since the Middle Ages there
had been a flow of live exotic
animals into Europe.*

famous but at the time it must have seemed extremely unusual for animals to be portrayed against a perfectly plain buff-coloured background.

In a very different manner, Reynolds was including pets into portrait painting. The delightful Miss Jane Bowles, aged three or four, sits cuddling her black and white spaniel. Painted in 1774-6 it is now in the Wallace Collection, London, where there is also a picture of Reynolds' mistress, Miss Nelly O'Brien, with a dog on her lap.

TRAVELLERS AND COLLECTORS

Although 'hunting, shooting and fishing' may have been the most often portrayed pastimes of the day, there was fortunately a more serious side to life. The more cultivated members of society regarded 'collecting' as a very serious activity as it demonstrated a man's curiosity and delight in his surroundings.

Travel, which led to collecting, was an essential part of a learned and cultivated life. The 'Grand Tour' of the continent, culminating in a visit to Italy, was considered a necessary part of a young gentleman's education, and many sculpture halls were added to country houses to display the classical marble figures acquired during these journeys. Some Englishmen returned home via Germany, in order to visit its porcelain factories, particularly that at Meissen, to purchase or order dinner services and figurines – including animals copied from those made by the Chinese for export.

Indian artefacts were still a great rarity in eighteenth-century Europe and, apart from textiles, had hardly been seen, let alone regarded as objects to be collected. However, the power of the British was increasing in India, due to political troubles and the disintegration of the Mughal Empire in the mid-1770s, and those Europeans engaged in colonizing the Subcontinent were in an excellent position to collect. At first they con-

centrated on the highly portable manuscripts and miniature paintings which were easy to bring home with them.

Warren Hastings, the British Resident at Murshidabad (1758-61) was a scholar in both Persian and Urdu, and dominated the British society in India intellectually. He encouraged other officials to explore Indian culture and collect its artefacts. Many of the resulting collections are now to be found in institutions such as the British Museum, the Bodleian Library in Oxford, and Edinburgh University Library.

Another British official, Lord Mornington, Governor-General of Fort William, set up an 'Institute for Promoting the Natural History of India', including an aviary and a menagerie, at the Governor-General's house at Barrackpore, near Calcutta. As the specimens arrived they were documented and drawn by a team of Indian artists. A duplicate set was ordered by Lord Mornington; 2,600 are now in the India Office Library, in London.

One of the most outstanding collections of Indian art to be found outside that country belonged to Robert Clive – or 'Clive of India', as he came to be called. Originally merely a representative of the East India Company, Clive later joined the Army and made his name in the British victory over the Nawab of Bengal at Plassey, southern India, in 1757. Lord Clive may not have been the most discerning of collectors (the treasures were probably obtained as booty or presents from native princes), but his son, the 2nd Lord Clive, who became Governor of Madras in 1798, and his daughter-in-law, Henrietta Antonia, greatly added to the collection. Among their most valuable acquisitions (on view at Powis Castle in Wales) are magnificent objects owned by the extravagant Sultan Tipu. The most curious of the Sultan's belongings is an animated carving of a tiger mauling a supine British officer, complete with roars and groans provided by a miniature organ placed inside it (see page 47).

MUGHAL PAINTING

'Prince Salim surprised by a Lion while Hunting'
(above). *This fine example of Mughal painting,* c.
1595-1600, shows Prince Salim turning to defend
himself from the lion attacking his howdah from behind.

Other miniature paintings, similar to this one, which
was sold by Christie's, London, are to be found in the
Victoria and Albert Museum, London.

INDIAN CRAFTS TODAY

India has held a magical fascination for artists for many centuries, the rich cultural heritage, spectacular buildings, the fantastic colours combined with exotic smells of spices and perfumes, and the overwhelming size of the magnificent countryside having a magnetic appeal.

The wildlife and the miniature paintings of the Mughal period have inspired three of the artists whose needlework is featured in this book (see pages 33, 43 and 45). If the Indian wildlife sanctuaries are not as well known as those in Africa it is because they are not so highly geared to the comforts of international tourists. Thousands of square miles are given over to preserving animals, birds, reptiles, plants and trees. In the past, the State Princes nurtured their forests to ensure they could lay on lavish *chikars* (hunts) for important guests and, although hunting and conservation would appear to be conflicting interests, they have been proved beneficial to one another.

It was not until after Independence in 1947 that the wildlife began to suffer, owing to massive deforestation and the fact that strict sporting rules were ignored to allow widespread poaching by villagers with guns. The tiger population dropped to a mere 2,400 animals. Now 'Project Tiger' ensures their safety and the best place to see them is the Ranthambore Tiger Reserve, Rajastan, originally the favourite hunting ground of the late Maharajah of Jaipur.

The Keoladeo National Park, Bhartpur, established in 1965, is said to be the finest bird sanctuary in the world, boasting overy 360 species. The Park centres around the freshwater swamp developed by the late Maharajah of Bharatpur for duck shooting at the turn of the century. Today the only sounds at dawn, the best time to visit, are those of birdsong and flapping wings.

India has been a favoured country for adventurous travellers over the centuries. However, it is no longer necessary to travel to buy Indian merchandise as it can be found throughout the Western world in department stores and specialist shops. The hand weaving, block printing and embroidery are such a refreshing change from the mass-produced, printed fabrics of the West. Imitation crewelwork curtain fabrics are still embroidered in Kashmir today for interior decorators throughout the world. The State Handicrafts Industries have done a marvellous job in keeping traditional crafts alive by encouraging production in remote villages and selling the output through their shops in India, and also for export.

Elephants, tigers and birds have always featured strongly in Indian art. Tiger shoots from elephants and horses were depicted in Mughal paintings, on carpets, and on embroidered *rumals* and *nazars* (covers for ceremonial gifts) since the early seventeenth century. The animals depicted in textiles are often auspicious symbols, many being associated with religion. For example, the fish – by virtue of its abundance in rivers and the sea – represents fertility.

The *dhurries* (cotton rugs) woven by long-term prisoners in jail sometimes show animals representing freedom, water birds flying in the sky and black buck roaming in the forest, reminding us of the 'emblems' of caged lions and knotted serpents embroidered by the imprisoned Mary Queen of Scots (see pages 22 and 23).

The age-old tradition of women embroidering dowry textiles for a girl from the day she is born has not completely died out, despite the fact that the dowry system is officially banned. Nowadays, the embroideries are also made for sale and are therefore, understandably, not of the same originality and quality as those done with loving kindness for a daughter or other relative.

The skill of embroidering *phulkaris*, the head coverings made for brides in the Punjab, has nearly died out, although old ones can sometimes be found in antique shops. Like paisley shawls, they make most decorative covers for furniture. They are stitched all-over on one side of the fabric,

generally with geometric patterns. Some, however, feature animals and may contain a positive menagerie; one splendid example includes an elephant, a deer, a camel, a horse, goats, a bush pig, a tortoise, a rabbit, a sparrow, a pigeon, a parrot, a cow, an owl, a peacock, a hen and her chicks, a fish, a frog, a cat and rat, and a small squirrel!

In northwest India, in the states of Rajasthan and Gujarat, the head coverings or veils are patterned with tie-dye designs made up of tiny white dots. These, too, are often geometric patterns, although old ones have peacocks, elephants, lions and tigers.

In Bangladesh (originally West Bengal) the traditional skills of weaving and embroidery go back to before the days of the Mughal courts. Their beautiful *kanthas*, lightweight quilts made with millions of tiny running stitches on fine muslin, are strewn with animals, arranged, in the Elizabethan manner, with little concern for scale. *Kanthas* were originally embroidered as gifts to be used against the cold in the winter months. Today they are made by women to earn a livelihood and, although the quality of the design has suffered, they are still full of delightful elephants, birds, fishes and leaves, all jumbled together.

TIPU'S TIGER

'Tipu's Tiger' (below), *possibly the world's best known mechanical toy, is a life-size carving in wood of a tiger mauling a British officer. A door opens in the side of the tiger to reveal a small organ, which can be used to play suitable music while the animal growls and the man waves a feeble arm and shrieks. The woodwork is Indian and the mechanism probably made by a Frenchman working for the Sultan, Tipu Sahib, of Mysore, 1782-99. It was captured at the fall of Seringapatam, Mysore, and is now in the Victoria and Albert Museum, London.*

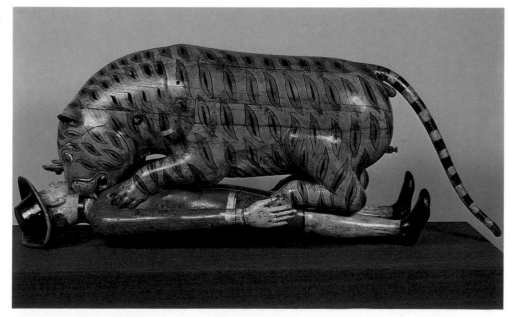

FOLK ART

'There are many who say that a dog has its day,
And a cat has a number of lives;
There are others who think that a lobster is pink,
And that bees never work in their hives.
There are fewer of course, who insist that a horse
Has a horn and two humps on its head,
And a fellow who jests that a mare can build nests
Is as rare as a donkey that's red.
Yet in spite of all this, I have moments of bliss,
For I cherish a passion for bones,
And though doubtful of biscuit, I'm willing
to risk it,
And I love to chase rabbits and stones.
But my greatest delight is to take a good bite
At a calf that is plump and delicious;
And if I indulge in a bite at a bulge,
Let's hope you won't think me too vicious.'

The Song of the Mischievous Dog, Dylan Thomas

GUATEMALAN BIRDS
by Susan Duckworth

Susan Duckworth's colourful birds (left) *were inspired
by contemporary Guatemalan embroidery.*

DOVES AND DOVECOTE
by Joy Hanington

Beautiful live doves perch tentatively around Joy Hanington's embroidered picture (opposite page).

Naïve or folk art has become so immensely fashionable it seems difficult to believe that even fifteen years ago hardly anyone knew what the term meant. The eighteenth-century paintings recording everyday life, and artefacts made by itinerants for ordinary people, have taken a long time to become so highly regarded and in the intervening years were ridiculed by practically everyone.

The journeyman painters ('itinerant limners'), and house decorator-cum-artists provided portraits, 'furnishing pictures' for the overmantels and overdoors of farmhouses. These included scenes in taverns, of boxing, cock fighting, ratting, and of the circus coming to town, and are now of great interest to museums, social historians, galleries and interior decorators.

Their work went swiftly out of fashion in the middle of the nineteenth century owing to the introduction of photography and the growth of education. Art schools and evening classes widened the appreciation of fine art, and this left folk art, which lacked perspective and bore no resemblance to the great classical paintings, to be scorned as something inferior.

It was a group of artists in Paris at the turn of the century, including Picasso, who first drew attention to naïve paintings when they 'took up'

Henri Rousseau. Self-taught, Rousseau painted by instinct, with a wonderful sense of colour, and was obsessed by lions and animals of the jungle. Similarly in Britain, in the 1920s, the painters Ben Nicholson and Christopher Wood discovered Alfred Wallis, a self-taught marine artist of St Ives, Cornwall. It is due to the patronage of their fellow artists, rather than that of curators or art critics, that the works of both Rousseau and Wallis now hang in national art galleries.

American collectors were much quicker than Europeans to appreciate the wonderfully truthful, compulsive and sometimes childlike qualities of folk art. They also realized its importance as a record of the nation's early social history. Many of the larger American collections of paintings and three-dimensional objects built up in the middle of this century have since been donated to major museums, where they form the nucleus of important collections.

The Whitney Studio Club of New York (now the Whitney Museum of American Art) organized one of the first exhibitions of American naïve art in 1924. Fifty years later it mounted a major show entitled 'The Flowering of American Folk Art, 1776-1876'. By this time interest was

CANINE FRIENDS AND FELINE FRIENDS

'Canine Friends' (above right) and 'Feline Friends' (right), a pair of mid-nineteenth-century English naïve oil paintings from the collection of Mr and Mrs Andras Kalman. On show at the Museum of English Naïve Art, Countess of Huntingdon Chapel, The Vineyard, Bath, Avon.

continued on page 54

DOVES AND DOVECOTE
by Joy Hanington

MATERIALS

Tapestry wool (see Colourways). The amounts given are for tapestry wool worked in basketweave or continental tent stitch. If the design is worked in half-cross stitch, 30 per cent less wool is required. Double-thread or interlock canvas is suitable for all three types of tent stitch, but if basketweave or continental tent is used an ordinary mono canvas may be substituted. Three strands of Persian wool or four strands of crewel can be substituted for the single strand of tapestry wool used for this design. (To calculate amounts for crewel or Persian wool see page 109.)

10-mesh double or mono interlock canvas 45cm (18in) square

Size 18 tapestry needle

Sheet of acid-free stiff cardboard or an artist's canvas stretcher frame to fit the finished embroidery

Scroll or stretcher frame (optional)

Tools and materials for preparing canvas (see page 111) and for blocking (page 112)

The finished picture measures 36cm (14in) square.

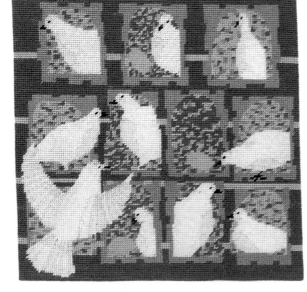

COLOURWAYS FOR DOVES AND DOVECOTE

Ap924	(Pa512)	a	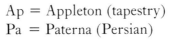
Ap921	(Pa202)	b	
Ap223	(PaD234)	c	
Ap203	(Pa486)	d	
Ap851	(Pa754)	e	
Ap555	(Pa770)	f	
Ap992	(Pa261)	g	
Ap752	(Pa964)	h	
Ap993	(Pa220)	i	
Ap991B	(Pa260)	j	☐

Ap = Appleton (tapestry)
Pa = Paterna (Persian)

YARN AMOUNTS

a	51m	(56yd)
b	40m	(44yd)
c	16m	(18yd)
d	9m	(10yd)
e	22m	(24yd)
f	4m	(5yd)
g	13m	(14yd)
h	10m	(11yd)
i	3m	(3yd)
j	39m	(43yd)

WORKING THE EMBROIDERY

Prepare the canvas and mount it on the embroidery frame, if used (see page 111).

Following the chart for the Doves and Dovecote on the right and using a single strand of tapestry wool, work the design in basketweave or continental tent stitch, or in half-cross stitch. Follow the colour key on the left when working from the chart. It is usually best to work all of the stitches in one colour before going on to the next.

BLOCKING AND MAKING UP

Block the completed work (see page 112) and allow it to dry thoroughly. Do not trim the canvas edges.

Lace the work over acid-free stiff cardboard (see page 115) or over an artist's canvas stretcher frame. The embroidery can then be professionally framed.

DOVES AND DOVECOTE
by Joy Hanington

These doves in their dovecote (left) are full of marvellous contrasts. First, there are the pure white shapes of the birds against the mellow, faded stonework. And despite their solemn air, there is something delightfully comical about the way doves poke their heads in and out of their homes before deciding to venture forth, swoop down and raid the vegetable garden, or wherever else they can find food. And what about the dove hovering in mid-air? Is it trying to decide if there is a vacant hole left to fly through?

Joy Hanington, the designer of this picture, is attracted to grand old houses with dovecotes – which are generally, she says, in a far more dilapidated state than the house itself. She enjoys using needlepoint to 'paint pictures' without getting involved with paint and brushes, as she does normally, as a painter, and finds it very relaxing to sit in an armchair, surrounded by a large selection of wool or cotton threads, stitching up her designs.

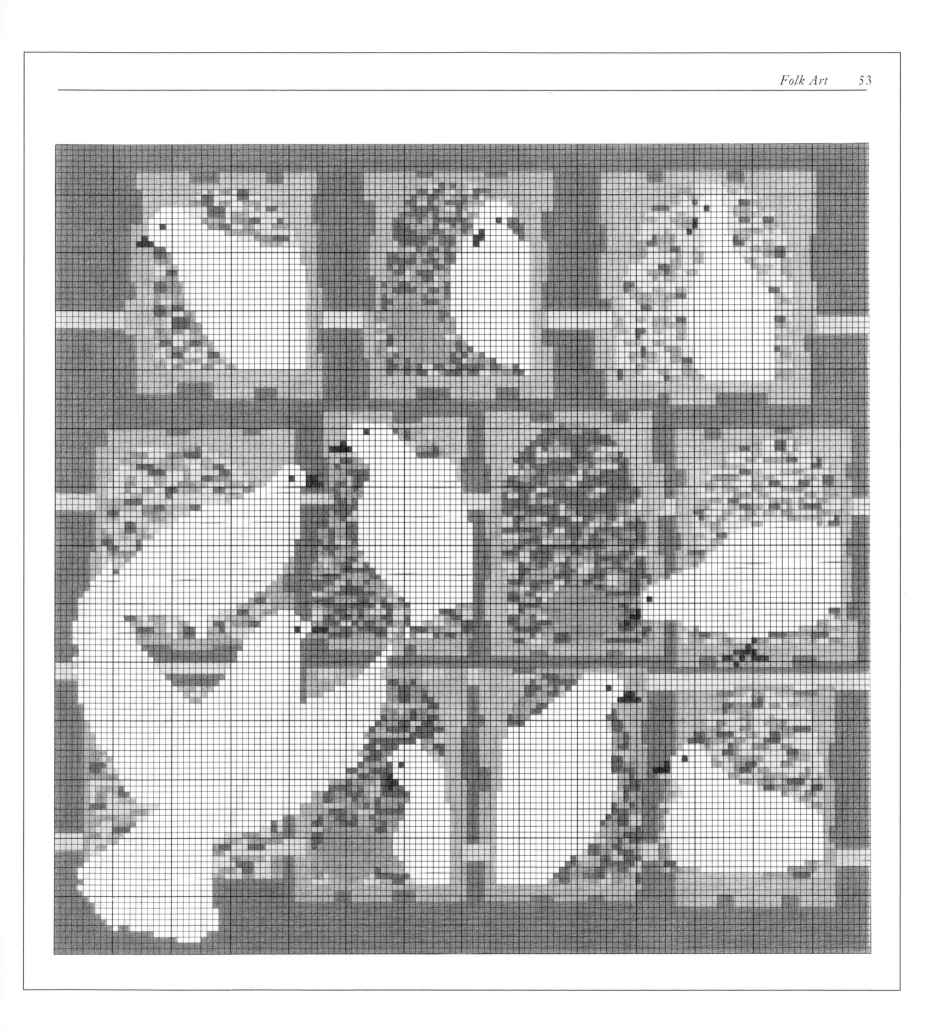

increasing in Britain also. The Crane Kalman Gallery, which opened in London in 1957, showed folk art alongside humorous modern paintings. Part of Andras Kalman's collection (which launched the gallery's still-thriving trade in this genre) is now shown at the Museum of English Naïve Art, in the Countess of Huntingdon Chapel, The Vineyard, Bath. In the same area, the American Museum, with its superb collection of quilts – another kind of folk art very much in vogue – opened at Claverton Manor, near Bath, in 1961.

Such events slowly drew attention to the charm of folk art, the popularity of which has now reached the point where it commands extraordinarily high prices at auction sales. The influence has spread to some trained artists, who have begun painting in the 'naïve' style – though whether they can ever quite capture the same childlike directness of vision as a self-taught artist does is another matter.

To find the best examples of contemporary folk art, one really has to look for work done in rural villages of Third World countries. In the state of Rajasthan, in India, for example, craftsmen produce delightful carved and painted wooden figures. Textiles, featuring printed, woven and embroidered designs, are among the most charming examples of folk art; a Central American fabric embroidered with birds provided Susan Duckworth with the idea for her colourful cushion design (page 59), and Lillian Delevoryas drew inspiration for her fish cushion (page 99) from a fabric hand printed in Africa.

RURAL LIFE

Animals feature very strongly in all forms of folk art, reflecting the importance and affection in which they were held by people living close to the land, and many British and American naïve paintings show the same characteristics. There are marvellous portraits of proud-looking people in their Sunday best clothes; farmhouses set in neatly tended fields with a small town or village and church filling part of the landscape; and seascapes. A different aspect of rural life comes in the scenes depicting the rather cruel side of everyday life in eighteenth-century Britain with cock fighting, replaced when it was banned with 'ratting' by dogs, boxing, and the field sports of hunting, shooting and fishing. Continental folk art appears to have been quite different, being largely devoted to religious subjects.

There is often more than a touch of earthy humour in the early English rural and hunting scenes painted for the farmer rather than the squire. In 'A Difficult Fence', a late-eighteenth-century painting, the huntsman is trying to pull his horse through a hedge – the horse having evidently refused to jump it. A fourfold screen, of 1746, with eight panels showing different sporting scenes depicts hunting, fishing, shooting, riding, cockfighting, card-playing, dicing and moonlight bathing – the latter including a voyeur peeping out from behind the bushes at the bathing beauties. In the hunting scene the fox is about to disappear down an earth, and in the fishing scene a heron has seized a fish from under the fisherman's nose.

The laws of perspective were never a strong point with folk artists and, to us, part of the charm of a picture may be that the fields appear to rest on top of the farmhouse, and the horses and hounds are all standing on their back legs, jumping forwards in an identical movement as in the 'Hunt and Full Cry' (artist unknown). In a 'Shepherd with an English Sheep Dog' (*c*. 1820) inscribed 'Josia Pepper' (possibly the name of the shepherd), an old man looks particularly miserable as lightning zigzags across the rain-filled sky. He is sheltering under a tree, with his dog looking anxiously up towards him. Three sheep are lying asleep on the other side of the shepherd, in this charming rural landscape of small fields with a building fading away in the background.

FOUR-FOLD SCREEN

A four-fold screen (right) *of 1746 with eight panels (six of which are shown here) showing different country pursuits, each a charming naïve painting in its own right. There is an earthy touch of humour to the eight scenes depicting hunting, cockfighting, shooting, fishing, card playing, horse riding, dicing and bathing. The screen is in the Victoria and Albert Museum, London.*

A FAT PIG
by John Miles

The picture below (c. 1820) is attributed to John Miles of Northleach, Gloucestershire and was lent by Iona Antiques (London) for the excellent exhibition 'This Land is Our Land' at the Mall Galleries in 1989, which celebrated the long tradition of British agricultural painting. The pig's owner, Mr Gillett of Sherborne, was clearly very proud of his mountainous sow and quite rightly too.

Another painting full of activity is 'Bringing Home the Cows'. Here, four cows – one white, one black and white, and two brown and white – walk in line towards a barn, with a smartly dressed farmer and his dog bringing up the rear. In a field across the hedge are sheep and two farm workers, one with a scythe, with more figures in the farm-yard and a milkmaid sitting beside a large pail of milk in the foreground. There is a total of eight people in one section of the farm, a very different tale from today when you would be lucky to see a lone figure driving a tractor.

There are, too, portraits of prize bulls and rams which were used to show off their stud potential at a time when British farmers were taking an interest in agricultural reform and scientific stock breeding. These often look comical as they were padded out to the most extraordinary shapes – enlarged by the artist as requested by the farmer-owner who wanted his animals to look fashionable so their services would be more in demand.

Edward Hicks, a devout Quaker and preacher of Pennsylvania, was the master of American naïve animal paintings in the mid-nineteenth century. He painted more than 100 canvases on the theme of 'The Peaceable Kingdom', with lions and leopards, bison, sheep, goats and wolves in idyllic landscapes. In these wonderful paintings, crammed with detail, the animals all stare forwards, looking extremely anxious, just as humans did in the early naïve portraits. His 'Noah's Ark' (1846) is based on a lithograph by Nathaniel Currier which Hicks has altered by turning the Ark into a Pennsylvania barn.

FOLK ART IN THE ROUND

Three-dimensional folk art objects are to be found in abundance in some American museums. These collections include such items as painted furniture, weathervanes, decoy ducks, ships' figure-heads and carousel horses carved by German immigrant woodcutters. Shop signs in the form of carved figures – Indians and blackamoors for tobacconists and Orientals for tea merchants – were useful as well as ornamental at a time when many people were illiterate, serving the same function as pub signs once did in England.

TWO DOGS
by Catherine Reurs

The Labrador and the English Setter on these cushions (right) are two designs by Catherine Reurs, a former investment banker from Boston, now working as a designer. Her needlepoint designs are all in the naïve, folk art style, using figures in a straightforward manner against a perfectly plain background.

Both dogs are great favourites with the English sporting fraternity – particularly the Labrador, which, being a steady retriever of game, is the favoured breed for field trials and for shooting. These wonderfully sloppy dogs also have a marvellously easy-going temperament, which makes them good with small children.

(A FAT PIG)
(Bred and Fed by Mr C. GILLETT, of Sherborne, near NORTHLEACH, ... AND ... Weighed 38, and 11.)

GUATEMALAN BIRDS
by Susan Duckworth

The instructions for working the
Guatemalan Birds (opposite
page) are given on pages 60
and 61.

Weathervanes come in a great variety of forms, and might be made of iron, by blacksmiths, or carved in wood and painted. Many represent real or imaginary animals, like swans, fiery-looking horses and sea serpents. A cockerel, representing the story of the denial of Christ by St Peter, sometimes appeared on church steeples, as well as other Christian symbols such as a goat, or even the Archangel Gabriel.

Then there are the decoy fish used for fishing through the ice in the Great Lakes – one being over 1.3 metres (4 feet) long. Carved and painted decoy ducks represent a wide variety of birds: bluebill drake, Canada goose, pintail drake, black duck and, among the shore bird decoys on stalks, are a sandpiper, dowitcher, black-bellied plover and sickle-billed curlew, to name a few.

Many early folk artists used prints and engravings as source material. The lion, so often seen in early English embroidery, is to be found in a marvellously bold tavern sign painted by William Rice in 1818 for the Goodwin Tavern, in Hartford, Connecticut. A similar lion is to be found on some painted furniture which was displayed at the 1974 Whitney show; and a lioness walks through a landscape painted on the top of a side chair. Animals and birds also feature in kitchen utensils, particularly the handles of pie crimpers. These were sometimes carved in the shape of birds from whale ivory by sailors on

whaling vessels, who were probably thinking longingly of a home-baked pie. 'Scrimshaw' work, as it was called, was a sociable occupation for men at sea for many years at a stretch.

RUGS AND QUILTS

Textiles, particularly American quilts, provide some of the most interesting examples of folk art. The surviving bedcovers, rag rugs, bed rugs and embroidered pictures express the way the early colonists, often living miles from anyone else, set about making decorative and practical articles for their homes. They demonstrate a real labour of love, for the makers, working in the evenings, would have needed to card, spin and weave the wool or flax to make fabric before they could even think about spinning and dyeing yarns needed for embellishment.

Bed rugs, heavy carpet-like covers to keep out the cold, were made from the eighteenth century onwards by the first colonists in America and appear to be indigenous. They pre-date patchwork quilts and have been confused with rag rugs made for the floor. There is no record of their having been made in Britain. These coverlets, embroidered with multiple strands of twisted yarn, were made from homespun, home-woven linen or woollen cloth and embroidered in wool threads, sometimes in pattern darning but often in looped Turkey work stitches, which would have provided extra insulation against the cold New England winter. The designs are generally similar to those of crewelwork 'Tree of Life' motifs, with meandering vines and fanciful flowers. Of the few surviving examples, most are signed. One rug, signed 'Catherine Thorn, 1724', includes horses and cockerels in the design.

Hooked rag rugs for the floor are far more common, and often feature both domestic and wild animals. They came into fashion in America

LION AND BEAVERS RUG

'Lion and Beavers' hooked rug
(right) from the collection of the
American Museum in Britain,
Claverton Manor, Bath. The
small red beavers indicate that
the rug was made in a fur-
trading district on the border of
the United States and Canada,
possibly upstate New York. It
measures 91 centimetres by 1.2
metres (3 by 4 feet).

continued on page 62

GUATEMALAN BIRDS
by Susan Duckworth

MATERIALS
Tapestry wool (see Colourways). The amounts given are for tapestry wool worked in basketweave or continental tent stitch. If the design is worked in half-cross stitch, 30 per cent less wool is required. Double-thread or interlock canvas is suitable for all three types of tent stitch, but if basketweave or continental tent is used an ordinary mono canvas may be substituted. Two strands of Persian wool or three strands of crewel can be substituted for the single strand of tapestry wool used for this design. (To calculate amounts for crewel or Persian wool see page 109.)

12-mesh double or mono interlock canvas 45cm (18in) square

Size 18 tapestry needle

45cm (18in) furnishing fabric for backing

1.5m (5ft) narrow piping cord

Cushion pad (pillow form) 35cm (14in) square

25cm (10in) zip fastener (optional)

Scroll or stretcher frame (optional)

Tools and materials for preparing canvas (see page 111) and for blocking (page 112)

COLOURWAYS FOR GUATEMALAN BIRDS

Ap502	(Pa590)	a
Ap623	(Pa833)	b
Ap554	(Pa771)	c
Ap471	(Pa727)	d
Ap505	(Pa900)	e
Ap753	(PaD281)	f
Ap436	(Pa681)	g
Ap823	(Pa550)	h
Ap998	(Pa220)	i
Ap965	(Pa200)	j
Ap961	(Pa203)	k

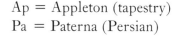

Ap = Appleton (tapestry)
Pa = Paterna (Persian)

YARN AMOUNTS

a	54m	(59yd)
b	5m	(5yd)
c	14m	(15yd)
d	9m	(10yd)
e	12m	(13yd)
f	12m	(13yd)
g	20m	(22yd)
h	16m	(18yd)
i	16m	(18yd)
j	29m	(32yd)
k	82m	(89yd)

The finished cushion measures 35×34cm (13¾×13½in).

WORKING THE EMBROIDERY
Prepare the canvas and mount it on the frame, if used (see page 111). Following the chart on the right and using a single strand of tapestry wool, work the design in basketweave or continental tent stitch, or in half-cross stitch.

BLOCKING AND MAKING UP
Block the completed work (see page 112) and allow it to dry thoroughly. Trim the canvas edges, leaving margins of 2cm (¾in).

From the backing fabric cut a piece 39×38cm (15¼×15in). Or, if inserting a zip, cut two pieces as specified on page 114.

From the remaining fabric, cut and join bias strips to cover the piping cord (see page 114). Make up the piping.

If using a zip, insert it in the back cover (see page 114).

Attach the piping to the back cover as described on page 115.

Join the front and back covers as described on page 115, and insert the cushion pad.

GUATEMALAN BIRDS
by Susan Duckworth

These highly colourful, almost comical, birds (left) come from Guatemala, in Central America. Susan Duckworth was looking through a travel guide to that country and spotted the birds on trousers worn by a peasant in a photograph. By using a magnifying glass she discovered the birds were not printed but embroidered on striped fabric – their decorative, slightly weird and wonderful shapes resulting from the freely worked stitches.

One of Britain's outstanding knitwear designers, Susan Duckworth originally trained as a painter, and has contributed many designs, including several for canvaswork embroidery, to the Ehrman collection of tapestry kits.

after burlap (jute sacking) grain bags began to be imported in 1850. The sacks were a perfect size for a hearth rug. The coarse, loosely woven canvas was nailed to a wooden frame to provide an ideal foundation for strips of coloured rags to be pulled through with a hook.

Designs were later stencilled on to the woven canvas but the most interesting and original rugs were the creation of their makers. The titles of the works are often self-explanatory: 'My Favorite Pony'; 'Deer in the Wood'; 'Our Pet Cat' (which looks as though someone has drawn around the sleeping cat). 'Our Pets' – two rabbits, two tiger kittens, a terrier and a group of sheep dogs; 'American Farmyard' with a building and a selection of animals which appear to be standing on top of the fencing! 'Peacocks' has a bird on either side of a basket of flowers, while 'Trotting Pony' shows a very sturdy animal moving at a brisk pace against a striped background.

The craft of quilting has been practised in many countries, but nowhere more enthusiastically than in nineteenth-century North America. There, the quilting 'bee' was not simply an efficient way to complete the quilting on a patchwork bedcover but also a means of gathering together country people living on isolated farms; like the barn raising it became one of America's great social traditions. Of the many varieties of American quilts made during the nineteenth and twentieth centuries it is the pieced, or patchwork ones, with their striking designs, that are most admired throughout the world. Many of these employ traditional patterns which were originally handed down from mother to daughter and are now reproduced in books. The names of many of the patterns used for these quilts reflect their makers' familiarity with farmyard and (at the frontier) wild animals: 'goose tracks', 'hen and chickens', 'bear's track', 'flying geese', 'duck paddle', 'turkey tracks', 'puss-in-the-corner', 'cat and mice' and 'hearts and gizzards'. Made of squares, rectangles and triangles, these patterns are extremely subtle,

NOAH'S ARK
by Catherine Reurs

The story of Noah's Ark, seen depicted in this embroidered cushion (right), *has fascinated artists throughout the ages and has been a particularly popular subject for children's illustrated storybooks.*

stylized evocations of animals.

The appliqué pictorial quilts, where the maker has fashioned her own templates, tell the liveliest stories. 'The Bird of Paradise' bride's quilt top of 1858-63, in the Museum of American Folk Art, New York, is a superb example. It consists of twenty squares and a border with animals, leaves, fruit and flowers all beautifully arranged in carefully chosen fabrics, predominantly of greens and reds, browns and yellows, on a cream ground. There are horses and riders along the border, pairs of peacocks, horses, turkeys, owls, and birds singing in branches or hovering over nests of eggs. Near the top on the right-hand side is the figure of a young woman. The accompanying young man, which exists only as a pattern cut in newspaper, was never added, nor was the top backed or quilted. The tragic theory is that the unknown maker's 'intended' was killed in the Civil War.

Quilts with naïve pictorial designs are much rarer in Britain than in America; however, the Welsh Folk Museum, St Fagans, Cardiff, owns a glorious appliqué quilt made by James Williams, a tailor, using leftover cloth from his workshop (see page 66). This mid-nineteenth-century quilt includes a variety of patriotic symbols and biblical stories: Adam naming the beasts; Cain and Abel; Noah's Ark; and Jonah and the whale are all contained within a dazzling border of zigzags and mosaics of red, white, blue, cream and brown, which give the quilt a look of the 1920s or 1930s.

Another tailor who fashioned pictures in felt, around 1830, was George Smart, 'Artist in Cloth and Velvet Figures', of Frant, near Tunbridge Wells, Kent. His rural scenes, with rather comical figures filling the foreground, tell of local history. There is 'Old Bright', the postman, delivering the mail with his donkey following behind, and Elizabeth Horne, the 'Goose Woman', in a large black bonnet and red coat going to market with a basket of eggs on her arm.

continued on page 66

NOAH'S ARK
by Catherine Reurs

MATERIALS

Tapestry wool (see Colourways). The amounts given are for tapestry wool worked in basketweave or continental tent stitch. If the design is worked in half-cross stitch, 30 per cent less wool is required. Double-thread or interlock canvas is suitable for all three types of tent stitch, but if basketweave or continental tent is used an ordinary mono canvas may be substituted. Two strands of Persian wool or three strands of crewel can be substituted for the single strand of tapestry wool used for this design. (To calculate amounts for crewel or Persian wool see page 109.)

12-mesh double or mono interlock canvas 60cm (22½in) square
Size 18 tapestry needle
60cm (22½in) furnishing fabric for backing
2m (7ft) narrow piping cord
Cushion pad (pillow form) 50cm (19in) square
40cm (16in) zip fastener (optional)
Scroll or stretcher frame (optional)
Tools and materials for preparing canvas (see page 111) and for blocking (page 112)

The finished cushion measures 47cm (18½in) square.

COLOURWAYS FOR NOAH'S ARK

Ap106	(Pa320)	a
Ap746	(Pa560)	b
Ap744	(Pa561)	c
Ap461	(Pa564)	d
Ap101	(Pa312)	e
Ap451	(Pa322)	f
Ap884	(Pa314)	g
Ap885	(Pa313)	h
Ap965	(Pa200)	i
Ap327	(Pa510)	j
Ap323	(Pa512)	k
Ap605	(Pa321)	l
Ap601	(Pa324)	m
Ap991B	(Pa260)	n

Ap = Appleton (tapestry)
Pa = Paterna (Persian)

YARN AMOUNTS

a	25m	(27yd)
b	46m	(50yd)
c	61m	(66yd)
d	16m	(17yd)
e	11m	(12yd)
f	35m	(38yd)
g	62m	(68yd)
h	12m	(13yd)
i	21m	(23yd)
j	29m	(31yd)
k	64m	(70yd)
l	54m	(41yd)
m	48m	(52yd)
n	30m	(33yd)

WORKING THE EMBROIDERY

Prepare the canvas and mount it on the frame, if used (see page 111). Following the chart on the right and using a single strand of tapestry wool, work the design in basketweave or continental tent stitch, or in half-cross stitch.

BLOCKING AND MAKING UP

Block the completed work (see page 112) and allow it to dry thoroughly. Trim the canvas edges, leaving margins of 2cm (¾in).

From the backing fabric cut a piece 51cm (20in) square. Or, if inserting a zip, cut two pieces as specified on page 114.

From the remaining fabric, cut and join bias strips to cover the piping cord (see page 114). Make up the piping.

If using a zip, insert it in the back cover (see page 114).

Attach the piping to the back cover as described on page 115.

Join the front and back covers as described on page 115, and insert the cushion pad.

NOAH'S ARK
by Catherine Reurs

Catherine Reurs has treated the story of Noah's Ark in the naïve tradition (left). Her animals have a simple charm and are lined up single file, rather than side by side. Is the lonely boat waiting for the animals, or are they already aboard and the ship about to be beached alongside the palm tree?

The colourings – pale mauves and blues – give the cushion an air of great sophistication that make it more suitable for an adult's room than a child's.

The chart (right) can be used in many ways. The individual animals could be enlarged and used on their own; equally, a strip of them could be used as a border around a cushion, or as a design for a belt. Those canvaswork embroiderers who prefer more realistic colourings, or brighter ones for children, would enjoy making their own selection of tapestry wools.

ANIMAL PATCHWORK
by James Williams

This remarkably modern-looking patchwork cover (below) *was made in 1842-52 by a tailor, James Williams. On show at the Welsh Folk Museum, St Fagans, Cardiff.*

THE HERITAGE TAPESTRY

Canvas embroidery is not generally a medium for folk art, unless you count the church kneeler designed by people who have probably never tried to draw since leaving school but have managed, often with the aid of a camera and a photocopier, to produce either scenes from their village or religious emblems and symbols. These thoughtful amateur efforts have often resulted in highly original and delightful embroideries.

One contemporary embroidery that will surely become a prime example of everyday British art of the 1980s is the 'Heritage Tapestry'. The ambitious idea for what is, in fact, a very large screen with fourteen panels, came from Kaffe Fassett, the knitwear and embroidery designer. Kaffe persuaded a British television programme to ask its many viewers to send in 15-centimetre (6-inch) squares of needlepoint canvas embroidered with a picture of anything they wished to celebrate, on the theme 'Count Your Blessings'.

Over 2,500 squares poured in from every part of the country, all designed by their makers, showing cats, dogs, birds and other pets, members of the family, houses, boats and lighthouses, flowers and gardens, hobbies, sports and many other subjects. Kaffe then had the difficult task of selecting 784 of the best and happiest of these folk embroideries, stitching them together and mounting them on the frame of the screen. The Heritage Tapestry is now on show at Chatsworth, in Derbyshire, the magnificent stately home of the Duke and Duchess of Devonshire. The remaining squares were made up into hangings for the television studio and for the Wool Marketing Board, who sponsored the project. Others, containing children's colourful embroideries, have gone to children's homes and hospital wards.

CANADIAN GOOSE
adapted by Ehrman

There is a splendidly surreal quality to this goose (right) *gliding past an urban landscape — the proud, majestic bird from the wild being oblivious to the rows of identical houses beyond. The design was adapted by Hugh Ehrman from an old hand-painted canvas that he picked up on one of his trips to the United States.*

The canvas is embroidered in tent stitch with a new flecked yarn developed in Germany, which gives a depth of colour and complements the warm, rustic feel of the design.

VICTORIANA

'Cherries fell in the orchard with the same rich
monotony, the same fatality, as drops of blood.
They lay under the fungus-riven trees till the hens
ate them, pecking gingerly and enjoyably at their
lustrous beauty as the world does at a poet's heart.
In the kitchen-garden also the hens took their ease,
banqueting sparely beneath the straggling black
boughs of a red-currant grove. In the sandstone
walls of this garden hornets built undisturbed, and
the thyme and lavender borders had grown into
forests and obliterated the path. The cattle drowsed
in the meadows, birds in the heavy trees; the
golden day lilies drooped like the daughters of
pleasure; the very principle of life seemed to
slumber. It was then, when the scent of elder
blossom, decaying fruit, mud and hot yew brooded
there, that the place attained one of its most
individual moods – narcotic, aphrodisiac.'

Gone to Earth, Mary Webb

*GLOUCESTERSHIRE
PHEASANT
by Ann Blockley*

*Ann Blockley sketched her subject from life for this
Pheasant design which has all the realism of a Victorian
oil painting.*

SHEEP AT CWMCARVAN
by Sarah Windrum

This intricate embroidery of sheep set in the Welsh countryside (opposite page) *is a very successful interpretation of the watercolour that inspired it.*

The Victorians were past masters at over-the-top decoration: plying pattern on pattern, borders on wallpapers, fringes on fabrics, overloading the mantel shelves with clocks and statues, china vases and knick-knacks of all shapes and sizes, and filling every spare foot of floor space with heavy furniture. Just as well they had armies of servants to do the dusting otherwise they never would have found the time to produce such vast quantities of Berlin woolwork.

The wives and daughters of the newly prosperous middle-class manufacturers and professional men had to be seen, for the sake of status, to have a great deal of leisure time. Time that could be employed by doing 'good works' and embroidering artefacts of every description to enhance their homes, from tea cosies to large reproductions of Landseer paintings.

At the beginning of the nineteenth century there was a fashion for 'needle-painting'. Realistic copies of Old Masters were embroidered with wool in long and short stitch on wool backgrounds to resemble brush strokes. The most famous exponent of this art was a Miss Mary Linwood who became a cult figure of the day, meeting royalty, and exhibiting her embroidered copies of paintings by the likes of Gainsborough, Raphael and Rubens in central London, Edinburgh and Dublin. Her copy of a Stubbs lioness, with a very

anxious frown on its face, was particularly fine.

Many amateurs also tried their hand at needle-painting, which in a way was a coarser version of the silk pictures embroidered in the previous century. A typical example was a pastoral scene of a shepherd and his dog guarding two sheep and three large shaggy goats, said to have been worked by the Duchess of Argyll around 1800 to 1820.

BERLIN WOOLWORK

Today we argue about the name for embroidery on canvas. Purists insist on the correct if long-winded term of 'canvaswork embroidery'. Americans call it 'needlepoint', and 'tapestry' is the most popular English term. Both are incorrect as 'needlepoint' is a type of lace and 'tapestry' is a woven fabric.

The Victorians avoided any such confusion, for them it was 'Berlin woolwork' – so called because a Berlin publisher, in 1804, began selling hand-coloured charts printed on square mesh paper. The patterns were worked in merino wool dyed to a great variety of brilliant, glowing colours. By 1840 the craze for this type of embroidery had almost become an epidemic in England and one trader, Mr Wilks of Regent Street, London, boasted of having a stock of 14,000 different designs. Later the charts were printed in colour as supplements in the increasing number of women's magazines.

Flowers, as in previous eras, outsold every other type of design. The Victorians favoured over-blown roses and circular posies of mixed flowers in brilliant colours. To achieve a realistic three-dimensional effect, plush stitch was occasionally used for the flowers. Adjacent rows of this looped stitch produce a deep pile, like that of a carpet, which can be cut when the embroidery is completed.

Plush work has a certain fascination and can be

VICTORIAN WOOLWORK LION

'Needle-painting' involved using wool stitches like brush strokes and was popular at the beginning of the nineteenth century, before the arrival of Berlin woolwork. This beautiful lion woolwork picture (right) *is in a private collection.*

continued on page 74

SHEEP AT CWMCARVAN
by Sarah Windrum

The finished picture measures 37×35cm (14½×13½in).

COLOURWAYS FOR SHEEP AT CWMCARVAN

Ap935 (PaD115)	a	▪
Ap715 (Pa900)	b	▪
Ap931 (PaD123)	c	▪
Ap962 (Pa203)	d	▪
Ap987 (Pa204)	e	▪
Ap711 (Pa923)	f	▪
Ap141 (Pa924)	g	▪
Ap205 (Pa872)	h	▪
Ap321 (Pa513)	i	▪
Ap762 (Pa442)	j	▪
Ap251 (Pa653)	k	▪
Ap691 (Pa455)	l	▪
Ap292 (Pa603)	m	▪
Ap356 (Pa601)	n	▪
Ap542 (Pa604)	o	▪
Ap991 (Pa261)	p	☐

Ap = Appleton (tapestry)
Pa = Paterna (Persian)

YARN AMOUNTS

a	3m	(2yd)
b	19m	(20yd)
c	21m	(23yd)
d	14m	(15yd)
e	7m	(8yd)
f	4m	(5yd)
g	32m	(35yd)
h	18m	(19yd)
i	32m	(35yd)
j	42m	(46yd)
k	22m	(24yd)
l	27m	(29yd)
m	54m	(59yd)
n	30m	(33yd)
o	10m	(11yd)
p	12m	(13yd)

MATERIALS

Tapestry wool (see Colourways). The amounts given are for tapestry wool worked in basketweave or continental tent stitch. If the design is worked in half-cross stitch, 30 per cent less wool is required. Double-thread or interlock canvas is suitable for all three types of tent stitch, but if basketweave or continental tent is used an ordinary mono canvas may be substituted. Two strands of Persian wool or three strands of crewel can be substituted for the single strand of tapestry wool used for this design. (To calculate amounts for crewel or Persian wool see page 109.)

12-mesh double or mono interlock canvas 50×45cm (18½×18in)

Size 18 tapestry needle

Sheet of acid-free stiff cardboard or an artist's canvas stretcher frame to fit the finished embroidery

Scroll or stretcher frame (optional)

Tools and materials for preparing canvas (see page 111) and for blocking (page 112)

WORKING THE EMBROIDERY

Prepare the canvas and mount it on the embroidery frame, if used (see page 111).

Following the chart for the Sheep at Cwmcarvan on the right and using a single strand of tapestry wool, work the design in basketweave or continental tent stitch, or in half-cross stitch. Follow the colour key on the left when working from the chart. It is usually best to work all of the stitches in one colour before going on to the next.

BLOCKING AND MAKING UP

Block the completed work (see page 112) and allow it to dry thoroughly.

Do not trim the canvas edges so that there is sufficient unworked canvas around the edges for stretching.

Lace the work over a piece of acid-free stiff cardboard (see page 115) or over an artist's canvas stretcher frame.

The embroidery can then be professionally framed at your nearest framing shop.

SHEEP AT CWMCARVAN
by Sarah Windrum

This pastoral scene of sheep grazing early in the morning, with sunlight slanting through the mist to make rings of silver around them, and the Welsh mountains in the background is based on a painting by Susie Martin, which was later turned into a large-scale needlework hanging by Sarah Windrum. The smaller version of the embroidery shown here (left) is set into a broad border inspired by nineteenth-century tapestry and worked in browns and greens.

Sarah Windrum is a full-time embroiderer living in Wales, who designs and stitches needlepoint embroideries of all sizes, from miniatures to large hangings. Many of her designs are interpretations of watercolours by Susie Martin.

THE NEW LITTER
by Arthur Heyer (1872-1931)

This is a perfect example of the sentimental but very appealing Victorian approach to animal painting (above). *Arthur Heyer, born in Germany, moved in 1896 to Budapest where he lived for the rest of his life. He specialized in painting animals, especially cats, and was much sought after as a book illustrator.* (Reproduced by kind permission of Newman & Cooling Ltd.)

VICTORIAN CATS
by Kaffe Fassett

Worked in twenty-six colours, this Victorian Cats cushion (opposite page) *is not the easiest of embroideries to work, but it is well worth the effort.*

quite charming when used for birds or animals (see page 87), but when it is used in aniline dyed wools of particularly hideous shades for a bunch of flowers, and the surrounding leaves are done in beadwork, the result can be quite horrendous!

Animals of every kind were depicted in Berlin woolwork. Fluffy cats were shown sitting on tasselled cushions, mice on piano stools, butterflies on tea cosies, and King Charles spaniels, the subject of endless pairs of Staffordshire pottery mantelpiece figures, seem to have been particularly popular; a special favourite was a goo-goo eyed one sitting on a silk cushion. There are woolwork pictures of dogs lying at their master's feet, a pointer putting up game for a gun, dogs sitting up begging and copies of Landseer's painting of Queen Victoria's pets.

The Victorians revelled in animal and sporting paintings, Sir Edwin Landseer being quite the most popular artist. Queen Victoria owned no fewer than thirty-nine of his oil paintings and sixteen chalk drawings. Landseer's giant paintings, such as 'The Monarch of the Glen', which shows a stag standing on a crag viewing his territory, were

immensely popular; engraved reproductions of them adorned the walls of countless homes.

Landseer began visiting the Highlands in 1824 and returned annually to stay with the landed gentry in their shooting lodges, which had been enlarged in emulation of the royal castle in Balmoral in the 'Scottish baronial' style. Highland scenes were among his best work. Queen Victoria made the Highlands fashionable and established a Scottish social season of parties and balls, concentrated around the start of the grouse-shooting season.

Landseer's painting is marked by its superb detail and tactile qualities and also, in many cases, by a large dollop of sentimentality. There is more than a touch of pathos, for example, in 'The Old Shepherd's Chief Mourner', with the dog leaning against a rug draped over his master's coffin. In 'Laying Down the Law', a large poodle sitting in a chair, his paw on the table, is the judge, and the twelve assorted dogs, most of them belonging to the Duke of Devonshire, who commissioned the picture in 1842, represent various court officials and jurors. Working in a more restrained manner, Landseer also made the sculptures for the bronze lions at the base of Nelson's Column in Trafalgar Square, London.

Engravings, made around the same time, of hunting, racing and sporting scenes are still to be found in English country houses. Winning racehorses were painted by John Frederick Herring, and Henry Alken depicted hunting scenes, with top-hatted huntsmen and ladies, riding sidesaddle, with hounds, charging over fences and ditches.

Did the hunting, shooting, fishing man really wear the slippers so lovingly embroidered with foxes' heads on the tops and bushy tails along the sides – or the tartan waistcoat with fox-head buttons?

The opening, in 1828, of the London Zoo (as it is now called) in Regent's Park, increased the interest in animal subjects and exotic birds. Parrots

continued on page 78

VICTORIAN CATS
by Kaffe Fassett

MATERIALS

Lightweight double knitting (or, in U.S., heavy sport-weight knitting yarn), which is a tapestry wool weight (see Colourways). The amounts given are for tapestry wool worked in basketweave or continental tent stitch. If the design is worked in half-cross stitch, 30 per cent less wool is required. Double-thread or interlock canvas is suit-able for all three types of tent stitch, but if basket-weave or continental tent is used an ordinary mono canvas may be substituted.

Three strands of Persian wool or four strands of crewel can be substituted for the single strand of tapestry wool used for this design. (To calculate amounts for crewel or Persian wool see page 109.) To achieve the best results use the type of yarn specified for the original. The yarn colours can rarely be exactly matched in another brand. In a design such as this, which uses so many colours (twenty-six), it is especially important to match the original colours.

10-mesh double or mono interlock canvas 45×55cm (17×21in)

Size 18 tapestry needle

55cm (21in) furnishing fabric for backing

1.8m (6ft) narrow piping cord

Cushion pad (pillow form) 34×45cm (13×17½in) (if this size is not available, make your own following the instructions on page 114)

35cm (14in) zip fastener (optional)

Scroll or stretcher frame (optional)

Tools and materials for preparing canvas (see page 111) and for blocking (page 112)

The finished cushion measures 32×43cm (12½×17in).

COLOURWAYS FOR VICTORIAN CATS

Rn80	(Pa470)	a	
Rn616	(Pa462)	b	
Rn82	(Pa463)	c	
Rn613	(Pa464)	d	
Rn11	(Pa441)	e	
Rn28	(Pa471)	f	
Rn104	(PaD419)	g	
Rn402	(PaD423)	h	
Rn401	(Pa493)	i	
Rn65	(Pa210)	j	
Rn88	(Pa211)	k	
Rn50	(Pa544)	l	
Rn47	(Pa546)	m	
Rn411	(PaD275)	n	
Rn410	(PaD281)	o	
Rn68	(Pa915)	p	
Rn83	(Pa935)	q	
Rn9	(Pa731)	r	
Rn10	(Pa442)	s	
Rn106	(Pa652)	t	
Rn33	(Pa634)	u	
Rn61	(Pa200)	v	
Rn60	(Pa202)	w	
Rn58	(Pa204)	x	
Rn1	(Pa261)	y	
Rn8	(Pa733)	z	

YARN AMOUNTS

a	38m	(42yd)	n	21m	(23yd)
b	15m	(17yd)	o	7m	(8yd)
c	14m	(16yd)	p	7m	(8yd)
d	4m	(5yd)	q	3m	(4yd)
e	8m	(9yd)	r	4m	(5yd)
f	14m	(16yd)	s	16m	(18yd)
g	7m	(8yd)	t	2m	(3yd)
h	7m	(8yd)	u	2m	(3yd)
i	9m	(10yd)	v	30m	(33yd)
j	4m	(5yd)	w	7m	(8yd)
k	11m	(12yd)	x	12m	(13yd)
l	2m	(3yd)	y	55m	(60yd)
m	3m	(4yd)	z	4m	(5yd)

Rn = Rowan Lightweight DK (tapestry)

Pa = Paterna (Persian)

WORKING THE EMBROIDERY

Prepare the canvas and mount it on the frame, if used (see page 111).

Following the chart for the Victorian Cats on the right and using a single strand of tapestry wool, work the design in basketweave or continental tent stitch, or in half-cross stitch.

BLOCKING AND MAKING UP

Block the completed work (see page 112) and allow it to dry thoroughly. Trim the canvas edges, leaving margins of 2cm (¾in).

From the backing fabric cut a piece 36×47cm (14×18½in). Or, if inserting a zip, cut two

pieces as specified on page 114.

From the remaining fabric, cut and join bias strips to cover the piping cord (see page 114). Make up the piping.

If using a zip, insert it in the back cover (see page 114).

Attach the piping to the back cover as described on page 115.

Join the front and back covers as described on page 115, and insert the cushion pad.

VICTORIAN CATS
by Kaffe Fassett

A Victorian scrap album picture of two tabby cats has been translated into this cushion design by Kaffe Fassett, who has added a delicate lace pattern for an even softer and prettier look. The Victorians tended to be over-sentimental about their pets, dressing them up with huge bows and sitting them on tasselled silk cushions. At heart, even the most pampered cat is a hunter – stalking mice and birds with all the deadly cunning of a panther.

*GLOUCESTERSHIRE
PHEASANT*
by Ann Blockley

*Instructions for Ann Blockley's
cushion* (above) *are given on
pages 80 and 81.*

were often given the plush-stitch treatment and
there is a firescreen design of one sitting among
flowers and leaves. The completed needlework
would probably have been returned to the needlework repository to have the plush stitches cut and
contoured to give the bird a realistic shape.

Berlin woolwork did not go out of fashion until
the designs of the Arts and Crafts movement
appeared in the second half of the century.

Patchwork was another popular form of embroidery throughout the century, and because it
utilized leftover scraps of material and worn-out
clothes it could be done in the humblest of households. The impressive silk and velvet bedcovers
with geometric effects created by diamond shapes,
or the traditional English hexagons, must, however, have been made by the prosperous. Other
very striking quilts were by a method known as

broderie persé, in which groups of flowers, leaves, birds or animals are cut from printed cottons, and applied to a plain ground. One such quilt of 1851 in the Victoria and Albert Museum in London is filled with all manner of animals, from dogs and bulls to camels and lions.

Quilts made with plain fabric, the pattern being created by small running stitches holding a layer of wadding between the two outer layers of fabric, were made on frames by women in the poorer parts of England, particularly North Country mining villages, both for themselves and to supplement their meagre incomes. The finest were considered to be those made in Durham – hence the tendency to call them 'Durham quilts'. Some of the designs created with templates, or drawn by professional quilt-stampers, with various patterns, were very elaborate and took weeks to complete.

ART NEEDLEWORK

Beginning in the 1870s there was a movement in Britain and in the United States, allied to the wider Arts and Crafts Movement, to raise the standard of embroidery. Known as 'art needlework', it encouraged the study of old and foreign embroideries, and mainly featured floral designs worked with free-flowing stitches in soft shades of vegetable-dyed silks or crewel wools. In Britain the movement was promoted most effectively by the Royal School of Art Needlework, founded in London in 1872 and initially presided over by Queen Victoria's daughter Princess Christian of Schleswig-Holstein.

The school (whose name was soon shortened to the Royal School of Needlework, or R.S.N.) employed about a hundred women – drawn from the ranks of 'distressed gentlewomen' – to embroider designs supplied by William Morris, Edward Burne-Jones, Walter Crane and other leading artists. These included large-scale hangings, friezes, portières, curtains, bedcovers,

screens, ecclesiastical vestments and altar hangings. The school also sold what we would call 'kits': designs for smaller-scale objects such as fire screens and cushions which were drawn on cloth and accompanied by threads for the embroidery. A small portion of the embroidery was usually already worked for the amateur to copy.

Other embroidery establishments were set up to follow the Royal School's philanthropic example. These included the Wemyss Castle School in Scotland (founded in the 1880s and, like the R.S.N., still in existence), the Leek Embroidery Society (1879), and Haslemere Peasant Industries (founded in 1894).

In the United States, a display of work from the R.S.N. at the Philadelphia Centennial Exhibition in 1876 aroused great interest. Another American organization devoted to needlework was the Deerfield (Massachusetts) Blue and White Industry, founded in 1896. This was dedicated to reviving the delicate style of crewelwork typical of that area in the colonial period, which had been worked in shades of indigo-dyed wool.

continued on page 82

A PRELIMINARY INVESTIGATION
by Mildred Anne Butler (1858-1941)

Mildred Anne Butler was influenced by the Newlyn School of artists and spent the summers of 1894 and 1895 in Newlyn working with Norman Garstin who probably introduced her to Impressionism and the benefits of working direct from nature. She painted mostly in watercolours and took as her subject matter the local countryside, fields and farmyards, the coast of Tramore in Co. Waterford, Ireland, where she spent her holidays, and above all the tranquil gardens at Kilmurry, the house near Thomastown, Co. Kilkenny, where she lived most of her life. Her picture (below) is in the National Gallery of Ireland.

GLOUCESTERSHIRE PHEASANT
by Ann Blockley

MATERIALS

Tapestry wool (see Colourways). The amounts given are for tapestry wool worked in basketweave or continental tent stitch. If the design is worked in half-cross stitch, 30 per cent less wool is required. Double-thread or interlock canvas is suitable for all three types of tent stitch, but if basketweave or continental tent is used an ordinary mono canvas may be substituted. Three strands of Persian wool or four strands of crewel can be substituted for the single strand of tapestry wool used for this design. (To calculate amounts for crewel or Persian wool see page 109.)

10-mesh double or mono interlock canvas 50cm (19in) square
Size 18 tapestry needle
50cm (19in) furnishing fabric for backing
1.6m (5½ft) narrow piping cord
Cushion pad (pillow form) 40cm (15in) square
30cm (12in) zip fastener (optional)
Scroll or stretcher frame (optional)
Tools and materials for preparing canvas (see page 111) and for blocking (page 112)

The finished cushion measures 37cm (14¾in) square.

WORKING THE EMBROIDERY

Prepare the canvas and mount it on the embroidery frame, if used (see page 111).

Following the chart for the Gloucestershire Pheasant on the right and using a single strand of tapestry wool, work the design in basketweave or continental tent stitch, or in half-cross stitch. Follow the colour key on the left when working from the chart. It is usually best to work all the stitches in one colour before going on to the next.

BLOCKING AND MAKING UP

Block the completed work (see page 112) and allow it to dry thoroughly. Trim the canvas edges, leaving margins of 2cm (¾in).

From the backing fabric cut a piece 41cm (16¼in) square. Or, if inserting a zip, cut two pieces as specified on page 114.

From the remaining fabric, cut and join bias strips to cover the piping cord (see page 114). Make up the piping.

If using a zip, insert it in the back cover (see page 114).

Attach the piping to the back cover as described on page 115.

Join the front and back covers as described on page 115, and insert the cushion pad.

COLOURWAYS FOR PHEASANT

An0381	(Pa410)	a
An3026	(Pa920)	b
An0340	(Pa870)	c
An0428	(Pa871)	d
An0348	(Pa722)	e
An0734	(Pa700)	f
An0726	(Pa755)	g
An0638	(Pa651)	h
An3101	(Pa652)	i
An0217	(Pa600)	j
An0215	(Pa603)	k
An0707	(Pa500)	l
An019	(Pa950)	m

An = Anchor (tapisserie)
Pa = Paterna (Persian)

YARN AMOUNTS

a	11m	(12yd)
b	12m	(13yd)
c	34m	(37yd)
d	13m	(15yd)
e	26m	(29yd)
f	40m	(44yd)
g	58m	(64yd)
h	22m	(24yd)
i	24m	(27yd)
j	6m	(7yd)
k	2m	(3yd)
l	2m	(3yd)
m	2m	(3yd)

GLOUCESTERSHIRE PHEASANT
by Ann Blockley

Pheasants have appeared in textiles since the first European tapestries and in their more exotic Chinese forms on eighteenth-century furnishings. Ann Blockley's bird has all the realism of a Victorian oil painting, an era when game birds were often portrayed owing to the gentry's fascination with the great shooting parties.

Walking in the countryside of the Cotswolds on an autumn afternoon, Ann Blockley, who is a watercolour artist and illustrator, came across a group of pheasants sunning themselves on the edge of the bracken. Not having her camera with her, Ann was delighted that the pheasants remained still long enough for her to sketch one of them: 'It was as though they were posing for me.'

Selecting one cock pheasant, with its gloriously coloured feathers, and placing it among the dried grasses, bracken, fern and fronds, she intended at first to use the composition as a watercolour painting from which to make some limited edition prints. Instead she decided it would be an ideal subject for her first needlepoint design.

Ann Blockley lives in a thatched cottage in Gloucestershire, surrounded by the countryside and is a keen conservationist, passsionately interested in everything to do with the country. She has designed postage stamps depicting the four seasons of the English hedgerow and has also recently written a book, Learning to Paint the Countryside in Watercolour.

ARTS AND CRAFTS

The influence William Morris and his colleagues were to have on the decorative arts during the latter part of the nineteenth century cannot be overestimated; and it says much for the quality of Morris's fabric and wallpaper designs that they are still in production – probably in far larger quantities than during his lifetime.

Morris spent his life crusading against the evils of the Industrial Revolution and the adverse effect that revolution was having on the working man's pride in his job. He urged a return to the traditional handicraft skills and craft guilds of the Middle Ages. One of his great disappointments was the failure to bring art into the lives of ordinary people; being hand-made, his papers and fabrics could be afforded only by the élite. Iron-

PEACOCK

This magnificent peacock (right) is a detail from 'The Forest Tapestry', designed by William Morris, but with the animals – a hare, lion, fox and raven – by Philip Webb (1887). It is in the collection of the Victoria and Albert Museum, London.

ically, now his designs are mass-produced they can be bought by the general public.

The Red House, designed for Morris in 1859 by Philip Webb, was to be furnished in medieval style, for which Morris and his colleagues had such enthusiasm, and it was his frustration at not being able to buy suitable furniture and fabrics that led him, in 1861, to found the company of Morris, Marshall, Faulkner & Co.

Stained glass was in demand for the spate of new churches being built, and also for old ones being renovated, and the firm's initial success was in providing very striking window designs in the Pre-Raphaelite style. The firm also designed and made ecclesiastical embroideries, furniture, and, later, wallpapers, fabrics, hand-woven tapestries and hand-knotted carpets.

Morris appears to have taught his wife, Jane, to embroider; and to improve their knowledge of different stitches they studied, and even sometimes unpicked, old embroideries. For the Red House they created a series of embroideries, based on Chaucer's poem 'Illustrious Women', and these were made in their own highly distinctive style to imitate tapestries. Both daughters became involved with embroidering for the firm, and May Morris, who ran the embroidery workshops from the age of twenty-three, continued designing and carrying out commissions after her father's death. Jane's sister, Elizabeth Burden, taught at the Royal School of Needlework.

Intertwining arrangements of flowers, plants and leaves, and complicated repeat patterns were William Morris's forte. He left the human figures, birds and animals incorporated in his tapestries, fabrics and papers to be designed by Edward Burne-Jones or Philip Webb. For example, 'Trellis', one of his early wallpapers, with roses winding through wooden trellis, contains birds designed by Webb.

In the late 1870s the firm produced a series of bird designs for patterned weaves: 'Birds', a double-woven wool cloth said to be one of Mor

The charming circle of birds with sprigs of blossom on this chair seat (left) is copied from a Victorian cushion in the Collection of the Embroiderers' Guild at Hampton Court Palace, near London.

The original is worked on flannel and on examination it appears as though the embroiderer must have had the most marvellous eyesight to be able to count the threads of the woollen cloth to know where to place the needle. In fact it has been worked by a method often employed by the Victorians for upholstery when they wanted to achieve a softer effect than is possible with canvas. This was done by tacking (basting) canvas to woollen cloth then embroidering through both the canvas and the ground fabric. When the design was completed the threads of the canvas were pulled away, one by one, leaving the embroidery on the cloth.

The chair seat design is true to the Victorian original; only the colours have been modified to make them less garish.

ris's favourites, was made for Kelmscott House, his new home in Hammersmith. Others in the series were 'Bird and Vine', 'Peacock and Dragon', and 'Dove and Roses'. Yet another 'Strawberry Thief' was a printed fabric.

In the very handsome 'Forest Tapestry' a peacock, hare, lion, fox and raven sit on a border of spring flowers, reminiscent of the medieval tapestries. The solid background of leaves is pure Morris, while the animals were designed by Philip Webb. For the 'Holy Grail' tapestry, Morris collaborated with Burne-Jones who designed the frieze of deer grazing alongside a river bank – Morris contributing the heraldic shields.

Dissatisfaction with chemical dyes led Morris to experiment with vegetable dyes in association with Thomas Wardle, a silk manufacturer. One of Wardle's specialities was hand printing tussore silk with outlines of Morris-influenced, or oriental, patterns, which were sold to be covered with silk embroidery and gold thread.

We now think of Morris as having simplified Victorian design by turning away from overfussy, machine-made ornamentation and returning to rustic values – as seen in his 'Sussex' chair, with its plain ebonised frame and rush seat. However, the photographs of interiors decorated by Morris & Co. indicate that they were often very elaborate and, by our standards, still overloaded with a profusion of pattern and heavy furniture.

COLOURWAYS FOR PANSY THE COW

Rn616	(Pa462)	a	■
Rn613	(Pa464)	b	■
Rn40	(Pa691)	c	■
Rn36	(Pa633)	d	■
Rn75	(Pa694)	e	■
Rn30	(Pa655)	f	■
Rn109	(Pa925)	g	■
Rn99	(Pa330)	h	■
Rn126	(Pa331)	i	■
Rn62	(Pa220)	j	■
Rn65	(Pa210)	k	■
Rn61	(Pa200)	l	■
Rn59	(Pa203)	m	■
Rn110	(Pa260)	n	☐

Rn = Rowan Lightweight
        DK (tapestry)
Pa = Paterna (Persian)

YARN AMOUNTS

a	37m	(41yd)
b	58m	(64yd)
c	13m	(15yd)
d	28m	(31yd)
e	25m	(28yd)
f	15m	(17yd)
g	3m	(4yd)
h	3m	(4yd)
i	3m	(4yd)
j	15m	(17yd)
k	8m	(9yd)
l	6m	(7yd)
m	8m	(9yd)
n	69m	(76yd)

PANSY THE COW
by Kaffe Fassett

MATERIALS

Lightweight double knitting (or, in U.S., heavy sport-weight knitting yarn), which is a tapestry wool weight (see Colourways). The amounts given are for tapestry wool worked in basketweave or continental tent stitch. If the design is worked in half-cross stitch, 30 per cent less wool is required. Double-thread or interlock canvas is suitable for all three types of tent stitch, but if basketweave or continental tent is used an ordinary mono canvas may be substituted. Three strands of Persian wool or four strands of crewel can be substituted for the single strand of tapestry wool used for this design. (To calculate amounts for crewel or Persian wool see page 109.)

10-mesh double or mono interlock canvas 50cm (19in) square
Size 18 tapestry needle
50cm (19in) furnishing fabric for backing
1.6m (5½ft) narrow piping cord
Cushion pad (pillow form) 40cm (15in) square
30cm (12in) zip fastener (optional)

Scroll or stretcher frame (optional)
Tools and materials for preparing canvas (see page 111) and for blocking (page 112)

The finished cushion measures 37cm (14¾in) square.

WORKING THE EMBROIDERY

Prepare the canvas and mount it on the frame, if used (see page 111). Following the chart on the right and using a single strand of tapestry wool, work the design in basketweave or continental tent stitch, or in half-cross stitch.

BLOCKING AND MAKING UP

Block the completed work (see page 112) and allow it to dry thoroughly. Trim the canvas edges, leaving margins of 2cm (¾in).

From the backing fabric cut a piece 41cm (16¼in) square. Or, if inserting a zip, cut two pieces as specified on page 114.

From the remaining fabric, cut and join bias strips to cover the piping cord (see page 114). Make up the piping.

If using a zip, insert it in the back cover (see page 114).

Attach the piping to the back cover as described on page 115.

Join the front and back covers as described on page 115, and insert the cushion pad.

PANSY THE COW
by Kaffe Fassett

In designing this cushion (left), Kaffe Fassett wanted to convey the feeling of a Victorian dairy sign. A love of pattern, both natural and abstract, characterizes the work of this most eclectic of American textile designers, and the bold markings of black and white cows standing in green English fields exert a special fascination. Kaffe's love of mosaics and of Victorian flower-decorated tiles inspired the intriguing border, with its random patterning and purple and pale yellow pansies, each one slightly different from the others.

THE GLASGOW STYLE

It was the Scottish architect and furniture designer Charles Rennie Mackintosh who finally cleared away the Victorian clutter. His beautifully simple, sparsely furnished rooms, often in pale colours, with everything harmonizing, were among the innovations in design that launched the modern movement.

Mackintosh made his name as architect of the Glasgow School of Art (1897). He and Herbert MacNair and the two Macdonald sisters, Margaret and Frances (who became, respectively, Mrs Mackintosh and Mrs MacNair) formed a group called 'The Four' and together created the 'Glasgow Style' which gained international recognition. Their work was particularly appreciated on the Continent, where it was accepted as part of the fashionable Art Nouveau style. The Glasgow Style was indeed similar, yet quite distinct from it, being much more controlled, and 'The Four' thought they were working to counteract Continental Art Nouveau!

Jessie Newbery, wife of the Principal of the Glasgow School of Art, was to become a major influence in embroidery due to her attitude towards design and by changing the way it was to be taught in schools and colleges. Her husband, Francis Newbery, created the first-ever embroidery department within an art school thus at a stroke raising its status to that of an art form in its own right. (It is now a B.A. subject at Glasgow and a handful of other art colleges in the United Kingdom.)

Previously, embroiderers had worked to the designs of architects, painters and pattern makers, and while William Morris and his contemporaries had certainly made embroidery an important part of interior decoration the success of their designs depended largely on the skill of the embroiderer working them.

At Glasgow, Jessie Newbery encouraged her students to produce their own designs. Her work,

like that of her pupils, notably the Macdonald sisters and Ann Macbeth, relied on simple, yet highly stylized shapes in pale-coloured linen cloth applied to plain linen grounds. She enjoyed incorporating a very individual style of lettering into her work, which with its thick, couched outlines, resembling lead in stained glass, made a striking effect. So, too, did the plain curtains, with appliqué friezes at the hem and borders, made by the Macdonald sisters for Mackintosh interiors.

Ann Macbeth, who ran the embroidery department of the Glasgow School of Art in the early part of this century, later retired to Patterdale, in the Lake District, where she embroidered two large hangings for the local church. These works illustrate how difficult it can be to put a date on an embroidery. The strongly influenced Pre-Raphaelite style would suggest they were made at the turn of the century at the latest, whereas, in fact, they were embroidered not long before she died, in 1948. They are, nevertheless, quite magnificent. One of them, 'The Good Shepherd', shows Christ surrounded by sheep with the dramatic hills of the Lake District in the background and, at the bottom, the musical notes of the stirring and quintessentially English hymn 'Jerusalem'.

PANSY THE COW
by Kaffe Fassett

Instructions for the Pansy the Cow cushion (opposite page) are given on page 84.

DOG BENEATH A TREE

A perfectly enchanting early Victorian embroidered picture (left) of a sheepdog seated beneath a stylized cherry tree. It is worked in silk and wool on felt, the dog's coat having a textured pile. The picture was sold by Sotheby's in December 1988 for the staggering sum of £5,500, against an estimated price of £500-£800.

TWENTIETH-CENTURY EMBROIDERY

'Beasts of England, beasts of Ireland,
Beasts of every land and clime,
Harken to my joyful tidings
Of the golden future time.

Soon or late the day is coming,
Tyrant Man shall be o'erthrown,
And the fruitful fields of England
Shall be trod by beasts alone.'

Animal Farm, George Orwell

FROG IN REEDS
by Angela Chidgey

*Warm, sunny colours are the hallmark of an Angela
Chidgey design like the Frog in Reeds* (left).

GEORGE AND RUFUS
by Ben Nicholson

Ben Nicholson was one of several leading artists commissioned to design furnishing fabrics for the Scottish firm of Morton Sundour in the 1920s. His amusing characters 'George and Rufus' (1938) are screen printed on spun rayon (above). The fabric is in the Victoria and Albert Museum, London.

The textiles and embroideries that enjoyed such prominence during the Arts and Crafts period seemed to disappear into pale oblivion in the stark Art Deco interiors of the 1920s and 1930s. The 'brave new world' of industrial design, with its gleaming chrome and glass, called for minimal curtains in beige or white. Colour, where it existed, was provided by hand-tufted rugs with cubist-inspired patterns.

During the early years of the century, however, art needlework continued to be popular and, until the upheaval of World War I, life in the great country houses in Britain remained unchanged. King Edward VII entertained the other crowned heads of Europe, most of whom were his relations, to great shooting parties at Sandringham, Norfolk, his country home. There 'bags' of 30,000 birds were sometimes recorded. The Game Museum, filled with stuffed animal heads, reflects the King's passion for shooting in Britain, Europe and India.

Far more delightful, in every sense, are the animals collected by Edward's wife, Queen Alexandra. She had a passion for miniature birds and animals carved by Carl Fabergé, the famous goldsmith and jeweller of St Petersburg. There are tiny frogs, parrots, cockatoos, flamingos, toucans and many varieties of dog, from dachshunds and poodles to collies and bulldogs, all carved in semi-precious stones, such as malachite, agate, jade and rose quartz, and set with diamonds and other precious stones.

It seems these little creatures were not too expensive as friends gave them to the queen as gifts. To add to the collection, the King asked Fabergé's modellers to come and make clay models of all the animals at Sandringham – from the farm shire horses, hens, pigs, turkeys and bull, to the dogs, including the Queen's pekinese. These were all made in 1907 in semi-precious stones, apart from the King's famous Derby-winning racehorse, Persimmon, which was cast in silver. The collection of over 300 pieces is in a display cabinet in what was the Queen's sitting room at Sandringham.

Queen Mary added to her mother-in-law's collection and, having an extremely discerning eye, secured two of the famous Imperial Easter Eggs made for members of the Russian royal family. Her son, King George VI, in turn continued the tradition by adding cigarette boxes.

COW JUMPED OVER THE MOON
by Julie Arkell

Julie Arkell's jumping animal (right) is completely different from anything else in this book. It has a magical, fairy-tale quality which, combined with the wonderfully bright colours, makes it immediately attractive to children. The artist usually works in papier-mâché making unusual sculptures, jewellery and vases painted in bright, vibrant colours. On learning that she did needlepoint for relaxation, Hugh Ehrman asked her to design something for the book and this remarkable cushion is the result.

MODERN STYLES

By the 1920s interior designers were beginning to make their impact and manufacturers had to improve the quality of their designs if they wished their merchandise to be used in fashionable houses and apartments. One Scottish firm, Alexander Morton, had been employing freelance designers for their furnishing fabrics and carpets for a number of years. Among these was C.F.A. Voysey, an architect and prolific designer of fabrics and wallpapers. In 1905 the company had produced its first printed textiles under the name of Morton Sundour. For this range, in 1929, Voysey designed a charming children's fabric called 'The House that Jack Built'. It is full of animals, including a cow, dog, cat, hare and rat, which, in the best Eliza-bethan embroidery manner, are shown larger than the 'house'. The artist Ben Nicholson also designed for the firm, and produced an amusing fabric called 'George and Rufus' (see page 90).

Just as the peacock had ruled supreme as an emblem of Art Nouveau opulence and sensuousness, the panther and the gazelle were the speedy representatives of the new order. Susie Cooper, the first female Staffordshire pottery designer and manufacturer, used a leaping deer as her trademark, and decorated vases with animals, including a gazelle, squirrel and fish. Other fashionable animals had to be equally streamlined, and elegant women liked to parade with their greyhounds or borzois. These dogs were also favoured by Chiparus, a manufacturer of bronze and ivory figurine groups, and by Lalique crystal.

PANDAS
by Lillian Delevoryas

A photograph of two pandas frolicking in a bamboo grove inspired artist Lillian Delevoryas to design this cushion (right). Since pandas are native to the Orient, she put them in a setting reminiscent of a large painted Japanese screen, with a plain gold background.

With their distinctive marking, pandas are the most universally appealing of the large mammals. This, along with the fact that they are an endangered species, surely influenced the Worldwide Fund for Nature (in U.S., World Wildlife Fund) to choose them as its international symbol.

A new form of embroidery was needed to fit in with the mood of light and airy interiors and it arrived via the sewing machine. Rebecca Crompton, a very forward-looking needlewoman and teacher, freed embroidery from the rigid formality of thickly outlined appliqué which had been fashionable throughout the 1920s by using a variety of different fabrics – silks, velvets, cottons and laces – together with hand and machine stitching. On her retirement in 1936, she took lessons from Dorothy Benson at the Singer Sewing Machine Company in London, and together they devised ways of producing fine, outline designs on organdie and muslin. Rebecca Crompton became the first person to use machine embroidery as an artistic medium and created some very charming and stylish pictures.

Other embroiderers also experimented with different stitches and materials to produce 'pictures', and by the 1930s a number of women were making their name as textile artists. These were early efforts at trying to 'loosen up' embroidery and use it in a more abstract way. The first pictures which appeared around 1910 had been comparatively formal, in keeping with other pieces of 'creative' embroidery – mainly in appliqué, being done for clothing, household linen, churches, the suffragette movement and trade union banners.

THE RETURN OF CANVASWORK

The 1930s also saw canvas embroidery coming back into fashion. Owners of traditionally furnished homes began embroidering dining chair seats and backs. Among the more distinguished embroiderers was King George VI who completed a set of chairs for the Royal Lodge at Windsor. (He, along with his brothers, had been taught the craft by his mother, Queen Mary.) Some canvases were specially designed by well-known artists such as Duncan Grant, and hand painted to fit in with colour schemes by needlework shops, which also provided the wools.

In the late 1940s, after World War II, women in Britain were encouraged by the W.V.S. (now the Women's Royal Voluntary Service) to produce embroideries and knitwear to be sold as part of the country's effort to raise much-needed dollars. Queen Mary expressed a desire to be involved and offered the carpet she had been embroidering since 1941. This was composed of twelve panels of different flower arrangements, one including a parrot, based on eighteenth-century designs, and

DIANA THE HUNTER
by Rebecca Crompton

'Diana the Hunter' (1930), machine embroidery on organdie (above) *by Rebecca Crompton. The work is in the collection of the Victoria and Albert Museum, London.*

measuring approximately 3 by 2 metres (10 by 7 feet). The Queen evidently liked to embroider each afternoon while one of her ladies-in-waiting read to her. The completed carpet was exhibited in the Victoria and Albert Museum, London, prior to being shipped to America via a free passage on the *Queen Mary* liner. It was exhibited extensively in America and Canada and finally sold, through sealed bids, to the Imperial Order of the Daughters of the Empire in Canada for $150,000.

The Festival of Britain, staged in London in 1951 to prove the country had recovered from the ravages of war and that industry was back on its feet again, provided a golden opportunity for designers to introduce a completely new style – one full of vitality and much needed colour.

Lions, unicorns, heraldic beasts and animals in general were much in evidence as motifs. Susie Cooper decorated each piece of the china she was commissioned to make for the Royal Pavilion at the Festival with a highly stylized lion or unicorn in white on a dark background of blue or burgundy. Professor Robert Godden of the Royal College of Art designed a silver tea set with the pot spouts shaped and engraved to resemble a snake's head and body, the tail used as the handle.

During the same period the Dovecot Studios in Edinburgh, Scotland, were weaving tapestries from the cartoons of well-known artists. Among them was a small panel by Edward Bawden entitled 'Farming', a bold animal design with placid cows, sturdy fowls and a turkey in reds, greys and ochre wools. For Josiah Wedgwood, the sculptor Arnold Machin designed an earthenware figure of Taurus the Bull, decorated with transfer-printed signs of the Zodiac.

KNEELER DESIGNS

It would be interesting to know just how many people have been introduced to embroidery through being bullied into working a kneeler for their local church. There must be many thousands who, having initially agreed – probably with some reluctance – to 'do their bit' to help beautify the church, find to their surprise and delight that they have become totally absorbed in this most relaxing and therapeutic craft.

In the 1950s a spate of kneeler schemes were initiated in Britain for the churches and cathedrals being rebuilt and refurbished after war damage. The blocks of colour created by kneelers hanging along the backs of pews, or placed in neat rows on the floor, make an instant, joyously uplifting impact upon anyone entering the building for the first time. By the 1960s it seemed as though every village in the country was making kneelers, the most successful being either in uniform colours with the choice of design in the centre left to the individual embroiderer, or those all worked to the same design. Animals often feature in these embroideries by virtue of their role in biblical stories or Christian symbolism: the whale, the donkey, the Lamb of God and the Dove (Holy Spirit) are recurring motifs.

There are no antique embroidered kneelers. The Reformation had removed all ornamentation from Protestant churches and it was not until the Oxford Movement reintroduced embroidered vestments in the mid-nineteenth century that ecclesiastical furnishings came back into use.

The first well-known kneelers were designed by

Louisa Pesel for Winchester Cathedral and worked by the skilled needlewomen of the Winchester Cathedral Broderers between 1931 and 1936. The stitching is extremely fine, being on linen with 18 threads to the inch. Symbolic motifs, coats of arms and small pictures were used for the 360 kneelers, 96 alms bags, 62 stall cushions, 34 long bench cushions, and borders for five communion rails.

The Winchester project set a very high standard which was followed, after the war, at Wells, Worcester and Guildford cathedrals, St Clement Danes Church, London, and Eton College Chapel, to name a few places in Britain, and at the National Cathedral, in Washington in 1956.

Ecclesiastical vestments, and furnishings in

continued on page 98

BUTTERFLIES
by Susan Duckworth

The random butterflies on Susan Duckworth's cushion (above) *create a kaleidoscope of overlapping colour.*

BUTTERFLIES
by Susan Duckworth

MATERIALS

Tapestry wool (see Colourways). The amounts given are for tapestry wool worked in basketweave or continental tent stitch. If the design is worked in half-cross stitch, 30 per cent less wool is required. Double-thread or interlock canvas is suitable for all three types of tent stitch, but if basketweave or continental tent is used an ordinary mono canvas may be substituted. Two strands of Persian wool or three strands of crewel can be substituted for the single strand of tapestry wool used for this design. (To calculate amounts for crewel or Persian wool see page 109.)

14-mesh double or mono interlock canvas 45cm (17in) square
Size 20 tapestry needle
45cm (17in) furnishing fabric for backing
1.5m (5ft) narrow piping cord
Cushion pad (pillow form) 35cm (13in) square
25cm (10in) zip fastener (optional)
Scroll or stretcher frame (optional)
Tools and materials for preparing canvas (see page 111) and for blocking (page 112)

The finished cushion measures 32×33cm (12¾×13in).

WORKING THE EMBROIDERY

Prepare the canvas and mount it on the frame, if used (see page 111). Following the chart on the right and using a single strand of tapestry wool, work the design in basketweave or continental tent stitch, or in half-cross stitch.

BLOCKING AND MAKING UP

Block the completed work (see page 112) and allow it to dry thoroughly. Trim the canvas edges, leaving margins of 2cm (¾in).

From the backing fabric cut a piece 36×37cm (14¼×14½in). Or, if inserting a zip, cut two pieces as specified on page 114.

From the remaining fabric, cut and join bias strips to cover the piping cord (see page 114). Make up the piping.

If using a zip, insert it in the back cover (see page 114). Attach the piping to the back cover as described on page 115.

Join the front and back covers as described on page 115, and insert the cushion pad.

COLOURWAYS FOR BUTTERFLIES

Ap209	(Pa870)	a
Ap446	(Pa841)	b
Ap753	(PaD281)	c
Ap625	(Pa832)	d
Ap555	(Pa770)	e
Ap861	(Pa855)	f
Ap935	(PaD115)	g
Ap823	(Pa540)	h
Ap741	(Pa563)	i
Ap524	(Pa522)	j
Ap882	(Pa465)	k

Ap = Appleton (tapestry)
Pa = Paterna (Persian)

YARN AMOUNTS

a	19m	(21yd)
b	18m	(20yd)
c	14m	(15yd)
d	26m	(29yd)
e	19m	(21yd)
f	9m	(10yd)
g	9m	(10yd)
h	16m	(18yd)
i	19m	(21yd)
j	13m	(14yd)
k	107m	(117yd)

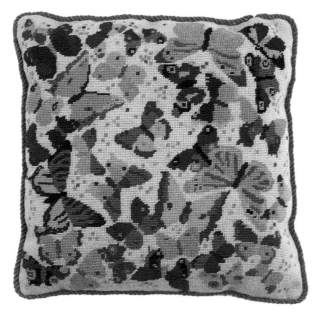

BUTTERFLIES
by Susan Duckworth

The butterflies on this dazzling cushion (left) crowd together to create a wonderful kaleidoscope of overlapping colour; and although the shapes may be true to life, there is nothing realistic about these creatures, which are intended purely as a pattern.

Best known for her knitting designs, Susan Duckworth does not mind whether a pattern ends up on a sweater or a cushion; frequently they are used on both. Susan Duckworth's fondness for intense colour can also be seen in 'Guatemalan Birds' (page 59), the other cushion she has designed for this book.

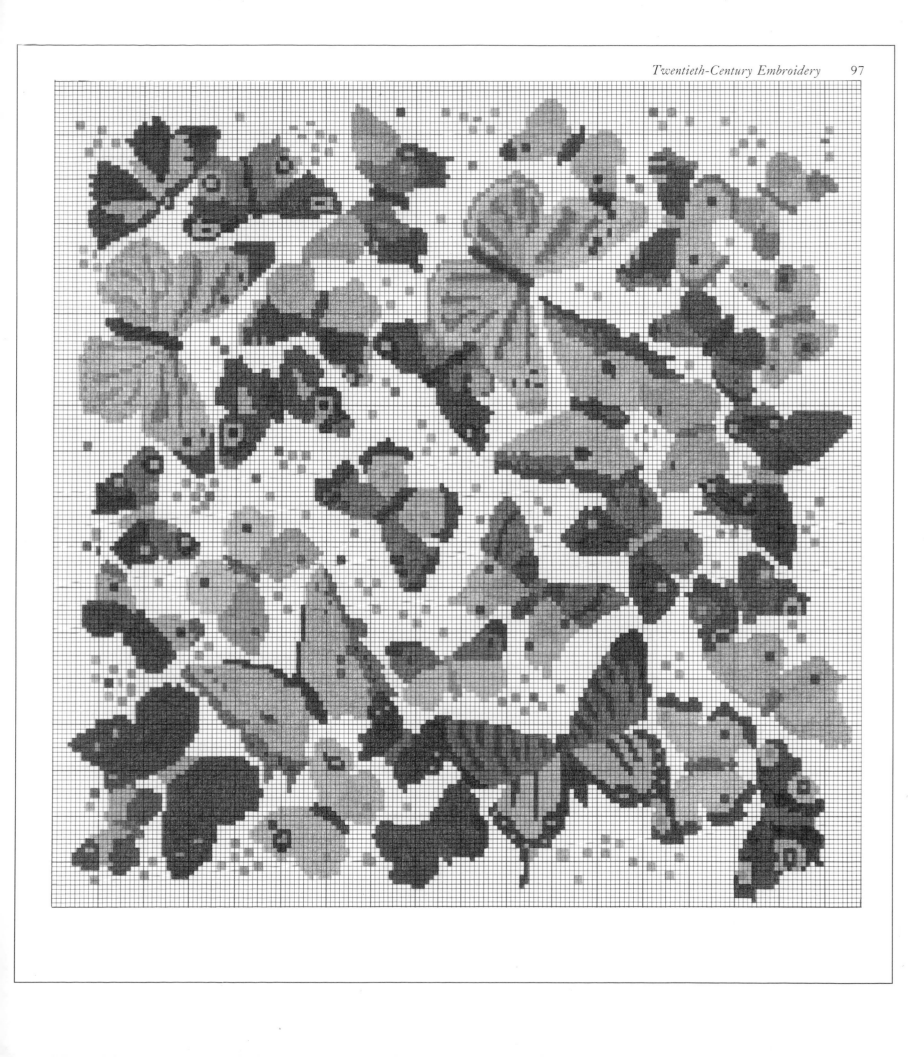

AFRICAN FISH
by Lillian Delevoryas

A length of hand-printed African cloth from the Gabon provided the design impetus for these tropical fish (opposite page).

NOAH'S ARK

'Noah's Ark' (right), *one of a series of samplers embroidered in different stitch techniques by members of the North East Branch of the Embroiderers' Guild in 1955. This one, in organdie appliqué, is by Gertrude Smith and is in the Embroiderers' Guild Collection at Hampton Court Palace.* (Photograph by Elizabeth Benn.)

general, have undergone a radical change during the past thirty years. An element of modern design has been introduced into cathedrals and churches by colourful and skilfully designed embroideries.

Beryl Dean has been a major influence in this movement and reigns supreme as designer. The 'Silver Jubilee' cope and mitre she designed, and made with the help of others, for the Bishop of London in 1977, the year of the Silver Jubilee of Queen Elizabeth II's accession to the throne, with appliqué images of scores of London churches in tones of greys, silver and gold is a masterpiece and can be seen in St Paul's Cathedral, London. Harder to view, as they are in the private St George's Chapel, Windsor, are quite magnificent panels with very dramatic figures representing scenes in the life of the Virgin Mary. She embroidered these in a variety of stitches and mat-

erials, completing them in 1973.

The majority of memorable and interesting embroideries made for public places since the 1960s have been stitched by their designers. One notable exception is the remarkable 'Overlord Embroidery', commissioned by Lord Dulverton as a memorial to the efforts made by the Allies to liberate Europe during World War II. The thirty-four panels, each 2.4 metres long by 0.9 metres high (8 by 3 feet), which make it 12.5 metres (41 feet) longer than the Bayeux Tapestry, show events during the war. It was designed by Sandra Lawrence and embroidered in appliqué between 1969 and 1974 in the most lively manner, using a variety of materials including battledress khaki and gold braid, at the Royal School of Needlework. It can be seen at the D-Day Museum, Southsea.

CANVAS EMBROIDERY TODAY

The most popular stitches for canvas embroidery through the ages have always been the flat surfaced tent and cross stitch. However in the late 1960s and 1970s, during a vogue for rough textured effects in furnishing fabrics and shaggy pile rugs, a variety of stitches were being used to create similar effects on canvas. Embroiderers on both sides of the Atlantic attended classes to learn how to do stitches with exotic names such as Algerian Eye, Gobelin, Tied Gobelin, Chevron, Jacquard, Byzantine, Leaf, Rococo, Smyrna, Herringbone, Double Cross, Long Legged Cross, Brick, and Chain. These were often worked into a square 'sampler' cushion composed of about twenty-seven squares, each containing a different stitch. As fashion moved away from abstract designs and textured surfaces, there has been a swing back to flat stitches which are more suitable for the figurative designs of today.

The establishment of art colleges around the

continued on page 102

AFRICAN FISH
by Lillian Delevoryas

MATERIALS

Lightweight double knitting (or, in U.S., heavy sport-weight knitting yarn), which is a tapestry-wool weight (see Colourways). The amounts given are for tapestry wool worked in basketweave or continental tent stitch. If the design is worked in half-cross stitch, 30 per cent less wool is required. Double-thread or interlock canvas is suitable for all three types of tent stitch, but if basketweave or continental tent is used an ordinary mono canvas may be substituted. Three strands of Persian wool or four strands of crewel can be substituted for the single strand of tapestry wool used for this design. (To calculate amounts for crewel or Persian wool see page 109.)

10-mesh double or mono interlock canvas 55cm (21in) square

Size 18 tapestry needle

55cm (21in) furnishing fabric for backing

1.9m (6½ft) narrow piping cord

Cushion pad (pillow form) 45cm (17½in) square

35cm (14in) zip fastener (optional)

Scroll or stretcher frame (optional)

Tools and materials for preparing canvas (see page 111) and for blocking (page 112)

COLOURWAYS FOR AFRICAN FISH

Rn602	(Pa920)	a
Rn78	(Pa872)	b
Rn403	(Pa883)	c
Rn20	(Pa865)	d
Rn601	(PaD211)	e
Rn93	(Pa322)	f
Rn53	(Pa503)	g
Rn501	(Pa341)	h
Rn122	(Pa504)	i
Rn90	(PaD501)	j
Rn417	(Pa663)	k

Rn = Rowan Lightweight DK (tapestry)

Pa = Paterna (Persian)

YARN AMOUNTS

a	35m	(39yd)
b	14m	(16yd)
c	9m	(10yd)
d	58m	(64yd)
e	38m	(42yd)
f	41m	(45yd)
g	44m	(48yd)
h	32m	(35yd)
i	32m	(35yd)
j	16m	(18yd)
k	18m	(20yd)

The finished cushion measures 43cm (17in) square.

WORKING THE EMBROIDERY

Prepare the canvas and mount it on the frame, if used (see page 111). Following the chart on the right and using a single strand of tapestry wool, work the design in basketweave or continental tent stitch, or in half-cross stitch.

BLOCKING AND MAKING UP

Block the completed work (see page 112) and allow it to dry thoroughly. Trim the canvas edges, leaving margins of 2cm (¾in).

From the backing fabric cut a piece 47cm (18½in) square. Or, if inserting a zip, cut two pieces as specified on page 114.

From the remaining fabric, cut and join bias strips to cover the piping cord (see page 114). Make up the piping.

If using a zip, insert it in the back cover (see page 115). Attach the piping to the back cover as described on page 115.

Join the front and back covers as described on page 115, and insert the cushion pad.

AFRICAN FISH
by Lillian Delevoryas

Lillian's niece, who worked with the U.S. Peace Corps, was with a team in Gabon setting up an industry based on fish farming. They managed to get a series of dams built, stocked with fish and, two years later, to see the fish harvested.

On her return she brought Lillian a length of hand-printed fabric from the region with a fish motif. The design, very lively and dynamic, was extremely sophisticated. The artist hung it in her bathroom where she could contemplate it while immersed in water.

When asked for a fish design for this book the African cloth immediately sprang to Lillian's mind. She extracted one or two of the fish, changed their scale and placement and worked out a watery background. 'The rest seemed to design itself,' she said.

BIRDS AND BEASTS
by Joy Clucas

*'Birds and Beasts' by Joy Clucas
(1950), using a combination of
machine and hand embroidery in
cotton threads on yellow felt*
(above). *Hand embroidery has
been used to give depth to the
animals. The work can be found
in the Embroiderers' Guild
Collection at Hampton Court
Palace.* (Photograph by
Elizabeth Benn.)

turn of the century certainly had a profound effect on the growth and appreciation of arts, crafts and industrial design. The number of teachers has escalated so fast that it is now possible to learn virtually every craft skill at full- and part-time courses and summer schools.

The colleges also, quite unwittingly, caused a split in the world of stitched textiles and since around 1910 two distinct 'schools' have emerged. On the one hand there is 'creative embroidery', as encouraged by the pioneers at the Glasgow School of Art and promoted in Britain today by art schools, polytechnics and the City and Guilds Institute. On the other, there is canvas embroidery, which is enjoyed by those who are quite happy to work other people's designs, deriving real satisfaction from having something to occupy their hands that will produce a pleasing result.

Today there is such an enormously wide range of tapestry designs available it is hard to believe that even fifteen years ago the situation was quite different. Charted designs were like gold dust and the design standard of popular kits was dismally low. The best designs were available, at great expense, from a handful of specialist shops stocking a limited selection of hand-painted or trammed canvases, and designs painted to customers' requirements.

Knitwear designers were quicker to catch on to the needs of the home knitter and patterns for high-fashion garments in exciting yarns were available long before anything similar was produced for embroiderers.

Since the early 1960s there has been a tremendous interest in canvas embroidery and, at first, a total frustration at the lack of designs that bore any resemblance to the wonderfully wide ranges of fabrics and wallpapers. A measure of this demand was demonstrated in the early 1970s when 25,000 readers of the British newspaper *The Daily Telegraph* responded to an offer for a black and white copy of a Berlin woolwork chart entitled 'Victorian Posy'. Admittedly it was published at a time when there was renewed interest in all things Victorian but, even so, it was an astonishingly high response. Fortunately the situation is now quite different. In Britain, Hugh Ehrman and a handful of others interested in promoting good embroidery designs have been commissioning and selling a great variety of interesting kits. In Hugh's case the business is mainly by mail order though he does have a very smart shop in Kensington, London, where customers can see tapestry designs stitched up and made into cushions or hangings. A range of exclusive knitwear kits is also available and the finished garments can be tried on.

One of the most interesting aspects of the Ehrman collection of tapestries is they have been designed by artists working in such varied mediums as oils and watercolours, papier mâché, knitwear and weaving. It was the 'Craftsman's Art' exhibition, staged in 1973 at the Victoria and Albert Museum, that finally succeeded in radically changing the image of the crafts in Britain from that of rather plain, serious and monotone objects (though often beautifully made in natural mate-

rials), to one of colour, wit, originality and excitement. The post-war generation of art college graduates had a refreshingly uninhibited attitude to design, unshackled by tradition.

Now the rigid dividing lines between art and craft have eroded to the point where, for instance, a ceramic artist who is in tune with contemporary ideas may be commissioned to produce designs for greetings cards, wallpapers and tapestries.

Unfortunately, contemporary textile artists, particularly embroiderers, are not so well-known as their counterparts in ceramics, jewellery and

furniture. This is probably because they rarely get enough work together to put on a 'one man' exhibition. The exception is Kaffe Fassett, the American embroidery and knitwear designer living in London, who was honoured with a show at the Victoria and Albert Museum in 1988-9. Kaffe's brilliant sense of colour and general enthusiasm for his craft have inspired a new generation to take up embroidery on canvas. His delicious designs 'Victorian Cats' and 'Pansy the

continued on page 106

FROG IN REEDS
by Angela Chidgey

The instructions for this design (above) are given on the next page.

FROG IN REEDS
by Angela Chidgey

MATERIALS

Tapestry wool (see Colourways). The amounts given are for tapestry wool worked in basketweave or continental tent stitch. If the design is worked in half-cross stitch, 30 per cent less wool is required. Double-thread or interlock canvas is suitable for all three types of tent stitch, but if basketweave or continental tent is used an ordinary mono canvas may be substituted. Three strands of Persian wool or four strands of crewel can be substituted for the single strand of tapestry wool used for this design. (To calculate amounts for crewel or Persian wool see page 109.)

10-mesh double or mono interlock canvas 50cm (20in) square
Size 18 tapestry needle
50cm (20in) furnishing fabric for backing
1.8m (6ft) narrow piping cord
Cushion pad (pillow form) 42cm (16in) square
30cm (12in) zip fastener (optional)
Scroll or stretcher frame (optional)
Tools and materials for preparing canvas (see page 111) and for blocking (page 112)

COLOURWAYS FOR FROG IN REEDS

An0133 (Pa541) a ▓
An0121 (Pa544) b ▓
An0564 (Pa553) c ▓
An0187 (PaD501) d ▓
An0185 (Pa522) e ▓
An3013 (Pa733) f ▓
An3229 (Pa735) g ▓
An0188 (Pa521) h ▓
An0730 (Pa583) i ▓
An3034 (Pa510) j ▓

An = Anchor (tapisserie)
Pa = Paterna (Persian)

YARN AMOUNTS

a 60m (66yd)
b 31m (34yd)
c 19m (21yd)
d 47m (52yd)
e 51m (56yd)
f 24m (27yd)
g 18m (20yd)
h 28m (31yd)
i 16m (18yd)
j 34m (38yd)

The finished cushion measures 40cm (15½in) square.

WORKING THE EMBROIDERY

Prepare the canvas and mount it on the frame, if used (see page 111). Following the chart on the right and using a single strand of tapestry wool, work the design in basketweave or continental tent stitch, or in half-cross stitch.

BLOCKING AND MAKING UP

Block the completed work (see page 112) and allow it to dry thoroughly. Trim the canvas edges, leaving margins of 2cm (¾in).

From the backing fabric cut a piece 44cm (17in) square. Or, if inserting a zip, cut two pieces as specified on page 114.

From the remaining fabric, cut and join bias strips to cover the piping cord (see page 114). Make up the piping.

If using a zip, insert it in the back cover (see page 114). Attach the piping to the back cover as described on page 115.

Join the front and back covers as described on page 115, and insert the cushion pad.

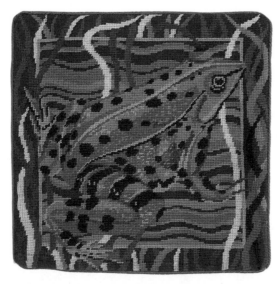

*FROG IN REEDS
by Angela Chidgey*

Warm, sunny colours of the Mediterranean are the hallmark of the watercolour paintings and ceramics by Angela Chidgey, an artist who divides her time between Siena, in Italy, and London. Hugh Ehrman first saw her work illustrated in House & Garden *magazine and asked if she would be interested in designing an animal cushion. She jumped at the idea as she has had an obsession with Africa and animals for years.*

Living in Italy at the time, she began to search the bookshops for animal references. The frog (left), sitting in the reeds with rippling water in the background, is based on a very small picture in a reference book on reptiles and amphibians translated from English into Italian. The border is influenced by the deep bands of pattern embroidered at the hem of old Chinese robes.

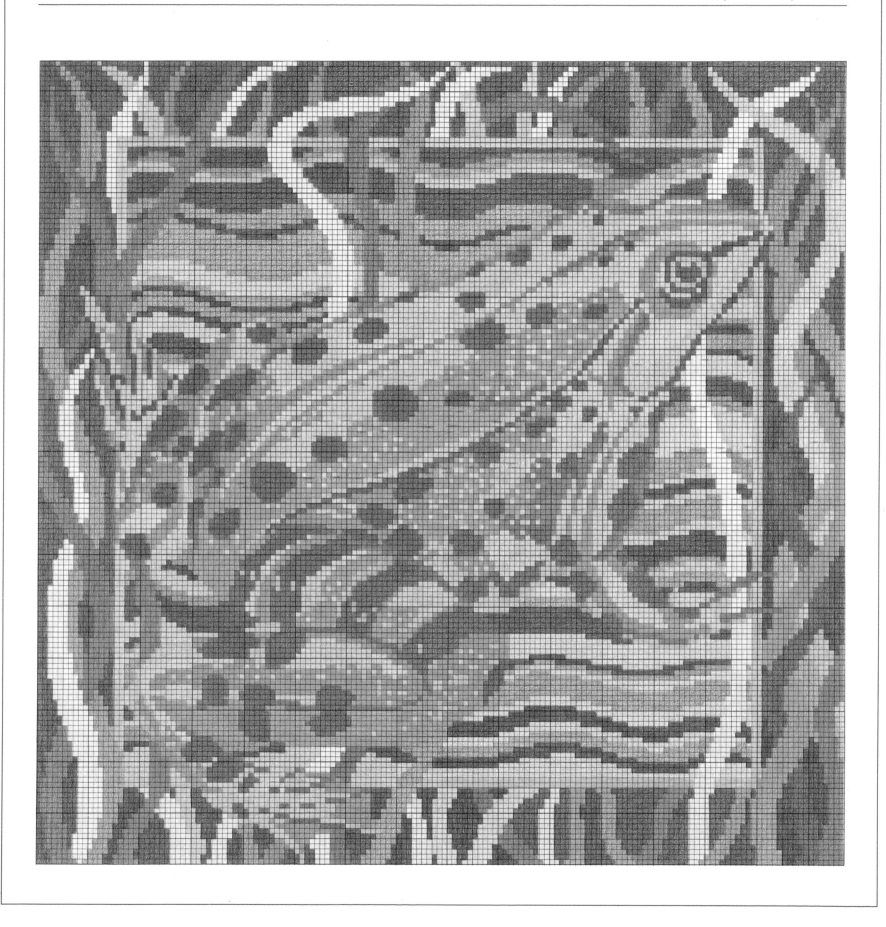

Cow' are charted in the Victoriana section of this book (see pages 77 and 85).

Several of the other contributors to this book have taken up needlework since being asked by Hugh Ehrman to design for him. As the artist Joy Hanington put it, 'It appeals to me greatly that I can sit relaxing in an armchair, surrounded by a wonderful selection of coloured wools, creating my designs without getting involved with paints or brushes.'

Animals have been a particularly popular subject with the artists represented here, whose enthusiasm extended to them offering more and more designs until Hugh had to say, 'Stop. Enough is enough!' Many of them live in the country surrounded by their own pets or neighbouring farm animals. Sixteen of the designs have been charted and all are available as kits. Whatever your taste and whatever your level of skill, there is bound to be a design in this book which will inspire you to pick up a needle and begin to create a work of art for your home.

LEOPARDSKIN CUSHION
by Candace Bahouth

Now that conservationists and the animal-rights campaigners have ensured that fake furs are far more acceptable than the real thing, it seems a splendid idea to stitch a fake leopardskin as a needlepoint cushion (right).

It may sound a crazy notion but Candace Bahouth, the designer, got the idea from the 'Tiger Rugs of Tibet' exhibition at the Hayward Gallery, London in 1988. The rugs, owned by the very grandest Tibetans, who used them to cover luggage on journeys, as well as to sit on, showed magnificent, rhythmical tigers in varying degrees of abstract design.

Candace, whose brother is Director of Greenpeace in America, loves the random spots of leopardskin and has several garments made from fabric she has stencilled with the patterns.

The cushion, which sits happily any way up, would look marvellous on an Art Deco sofa, a Mies van der Rohe 'Barcelona' black leather and chrome chair, or in any 1930s-inspired interior.

TWO PUNKS
by Candace Bahouth

'Girl Punk' and 'Boy Punk' (1981), two woven tapestry portraits by Candace Bahouth (right and above), the textile artist of international repute who designed the marvellous 'Hunting Rug' shown on the cover and in the Early Textiles section, and the leopardskin cushion in this section.

TECHNIQUES

MATERIALS FOR CANVASWORK

For embroidery on canvas you need only very basic materials: the canvas itself, thread in all the colours of the design and a suitable needle.

CANVAS

Originally the canvas used for this work was made of hemp; in fact, the word 'canvas' is derived from the Greek word for hemp, *kannabis*. Later it was made of linen. Today, the best canvas that is readily available is made of cotton; and in some countries you can find extra-fine canvas made of silk threads. Cheaper synthetic canvas is also available; and there is also a moulded plastic mesh, for small items such as coasters and boxes.

Conventional woven canvas is available in two main types: single thread, or mono, and double-thread, or Penelope. Single-thread is the more commonly used; it is suitable for any stitch and easy to work on because of the clarity of the mesh. Ordinary single canvas has a simple over-and-under weave, which has a tendency to become distorted through handling. This can be prevented to a great extent by using a frame, and it can also be corrected during the blocking process. Some stitches, such as basketweave tent and cross stitch, distort the canvas less than others, such as continental tent stitch.

A special kind of mono canvas, called interlock, is more stable. Its lengthwise threads are really double threads twisted tightly together; they hold the cross threads firmly, reducing distortion.

In double-thread canvas, pairs of threads are woven together to produce an extra-firm fabric. This firmer construction permits you to jump from one part of the design to another; where the areas of stitching meet the joins will be imperceptible. By pushing the double threads apart gently with the needle, you can work areas of fine detail with four times as many stitches as when working over the double threads.

Canvas comes in a wide range of sizes, referred to as the 'mesh' or 'gauge'. These have not yet been metricated: 14-mesh (or gauge) and 16-mesh, for example, refer to canvas having 14 and 16 holes (or threads) per inch. For cushions, belts and chair seats the most frequently used mesh is 10 to 14; for smaller items, such as evening bags, 16- or 18-mesh is suitable. For rugs, a double-thread rug canvas with 7 or even 5 holes per inch is normally used.

Canvas also comes in a variety of colours, with pastel shades, especially beige, being the most common. Because even with the most careful stitching minute amounts of canvas will show, choose a shade suitable for the colours in the design. Always buy good-quality canvas. Avoid any knots or thin spots; it may damage the embroidery threads and will not wear well.

THREADS

The threads most often used are made of pure wool and are spun specially for embroidery, being less stretchy than knitting yarns.

Tapestry (or tapisserie) wool is a smooth, four-ply yarn. Used in a single strand it is suitable for medium mesh (10-14 holes) canvas. Some brands are slightly thicker than others.

Crewel wool is a thin, two-ply yarn generally used with two or more strands in the needle. Being soft and fine (yet strong), it blends smoothly. Two or three colours can be used together in the needle for subtle shading.

Persian wool is another two-ply yarn, somewhat thicker than crewel. It comes in a triple strand, which can easily be separated to give one or two strands as required.

For a glossy effect cotton threads can be used. A single strand of no. 3 perlé cotton works well on 16-mesh canvas; no. 5 on 18-mesh. A small amount of a cotton thread can provide an attractive accent in an area stitched mainly in wool.

Tapestry wool has been specified for the projects in this book. However, you can usually substitute crewel or Persian wool if you prefer. The shade numbers for Appleton's crewel are the same as for their tapestry yarn. Close equivalent shades have been suggested for the Paterna Persian yarn.

You will need to calculate the amounts of the substitute yarn yourself, basing these on the supplied lengths of tapestry yarn.

CREWEL YARN

One hank of Appleton's crewel wool contains 190m (209yd); a skein contains 30m (33yd). The first step in converting from tapestry to crewel yarn is to multiply the length given for the tapestry yarn by the number of strands required of crewel. For example, if you need 121m (132yd) of tapestry and three times the number of strands of crewel, the total length required is 363m (396yd). Divide this total by the amount in a hank to get the number of hanks you will need: 363m (396yd) ÷ 190m (209yd) = 1.9 (1.89), or 2 hanks. If the total length of crewel required is considerably less than the amount in a hank, divide it by the amount in a skein to get the number of skeins required. However, hanks are more economical and easier to use, so it will be worthwhile buying a hank unless the required amount is only one or two skeins.

PERSIAN YARN

One skein of Paterna Persian yarn contains 7.4m (8yd); however, the strands are treble, so the true length is 22.2m (24yd). If two strands of Persian yarn can be substituted for one of tapestry, the required length given for tapestry must first be doubled. For example, 121m (132yd) of tapestry will equal 242m (264yd) of Persian. Divide this figure by the amount in a skein to get the number of skeins you will need: 242m (264yd) ÷ 22.2m (24yd) = 10.9 (11), or 11 skeins.

In some places you can buy Persian yarn by the 85cm (34 inches) strand, with a total length of 255cm (102 inches). First multiply the number of metres or yards required by 100 or 36, respectively, to get the total length in centimetres (inches), then divide by 255cm (102 inches) to get the number of treble strands required.

Note The yarn amounts given in this book have deliberately been rounded up slightly, to allow for individual variation in tension and the occasional mistake. It is far better to have a little yarn left over (which you can always give to a local charity if you have no use for it) than to run out.

NEEDLES

A tapestry needle has a blunt end which slips easily through the canvas mesh without snagging. Needles come in a wide range of sizes; the higher the number, the finer the needle. For 10- to 14-mesh canvas, a size 18 needle is most suitable.

FRAMES

It is quite possible to do good work without a frame, provided you stitch with an even tension. However, certain stitches will distort the work, no matter how skilled the embroiderer. A frame will help to keep the canvas threads properly aligned, and reduce the correction required in the blocking. It will also prevent your over-handling the work and so keep it cleaner.

A ring-type frame cannot be used, as the canvas is too thick to fit between the two rings, but a stretcher frame – the kind used to support the canvas of oil paintings – is perfectly suitable. The stretchers, strips of moulding with mitred corners, are available from art supply shops and come in many different lengths. Buy two each of the required length and width of your canvas and assemble the frame by slotting the corner edges together. Remember that the design must fit within the *inner* edges of the frame, so buy the stretchers according to the measurement on the inner edge.

The method of mounting a canvas on a stretcher frame is shown on page 111. A more sophisticated frame, the adjustable scroll frame, is expensive but can accommodate various sizes of canvas.

OTHER EQUIPMENT

You will also need two pairs of scissors: large dressmaking shears for cutting the canvas and small embroidery scissors for cutting threads. Tweezers are useful for removing mistakes. You may also want a needle-threader and a thimble.

TRANSFERRING THE DESIGN

If you have purchased a tapestry kit, you will find that the design will normally have been printed onto the canvas in colours matching or nearly matching the threads to be used. All you have to do is the stitching.

Designs given in books and magazines may be in the form of a chart or in the form of a drawing or painting to be traced onto the canvas.

FOLLOWING A CHART

There are basically two kinds of chart used for canvaswork designs: box charts and line charts. On a box chart (the kind used in this book) each square represents one canvas mesh or intersection. This type of chart is most appropriate for designs worked entirely in tent or half-cross stitch (see page 113); in such cases the squares can be thought of as representing individual stitches. As on a line chart, the thread colours can be indicated either by symbols or by actual colours.

A design given in chart form can easily be varied in scale by choosing a larger- or smaller-mesh canvas.

ENLARGING A DESIGN

In some books you may find a design that needs to be traced onto the canvas. If it needs to be enlarged first, it will usually be printed with a grid superimposed on it. All you have to do is draw a grid containing the same number of squares as the grid covering the design, but making the squares the appropriate size. Now copy the design freehand, using the lines of the grid as guides to positioning the various parts of the design.

You can easily enlarge any motif or drawing to a size of your own choosing. First trace the design from the original and draw a grid to cover it.

Draw a diagonal line from the lower left through the upper right corner of the tracing to create the enlarged outline as shown. Remove the tracing, construct the new grid, and copy the design as described below.

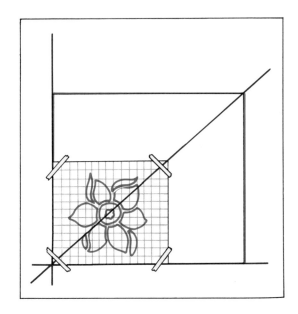

TRACING THE DESIGN ONTO CANVAS

Tape the canvas to the design, or hold it in place with weights. With a waterproof pen specially made for marking canvas (available from the needlework shops), trace the four edges of the design, running the pen along the groove between two canvas threads. Then trace the design itself. Follow any curved or diagonal lines freely; don't attempt to follow the grid of the canvas.

Allow the ink to dry thoroughly for several hours before beginning to stitch.

If you like, you can paint the colours onto the canvas, as is done for most hand-painted kits. Do not use watercolours, as these will run during the blocking process; even acrylics sometimes run, so avoid these, too. Use oil paints in a few basic colours, and mix these to get the required shades.

Add a little turpentine and mix well. Test the consistency on some spare canvas: the colour should be bright and the paint just thin enough so that it doesn't clog the canvas mesh. The paint may take two or three days to dry.

PREPARING THE CANVAS

Cut the canvas 4-5cm (2 inches) larger all round than the size of the finished work. Bind the edges with masking tape to prevent them from unravelling, or machine stitch lengths of seam binding over the edges.

Place the canvas on a piece of sturdy paper, such as blotting paper, and draw round the edges with a pencil. Keep this outline for use later when blocking the completed canvas.

As you are working from a chart, mark the vertical and horizontal centres of the canvas. The chart's centre should be marked with a cross. If this cross lies between stitches, mark the canvas between two threads either with a waterproof canvas-marking pen or with tacking (basting). If the centre of the chart runs along a line of stitches, run the pen straight along a canvas thread at the vertical and horizontal centres. Begin stitching at the centre point of the design.

MOUNTING THE CANVAS ON A
STRETCHER FRAME

Once the design has been transferred, or the centre marked, the canvas may be mounted onto a frame.

Unless you are going to be undertaking a great deal of canvaswork of different sizes, a stretcher frame is perfectly suitable. You will need to buy four stretchers, two each of the required length and width for your canvas.

To mount your prepared canvas, first mark the centre point on each side of the frame, and on each side of the canvas. Match the centre mark of the top edge of the canvas to the corresponding mark on the frame, and fix it in place with drawing pins

(thumbtacks).

Working outwards to the edges, fasten the top edge of the canvas to the frame, placing the pins (tacks) about 2cm (¾ inches) apart. Repeat along the bottom edge, pulling the canvas taut.

When fastening the side edges, begin by fixing the centre points as before, then work on one side, then the other, from the centre to the edges, plac-

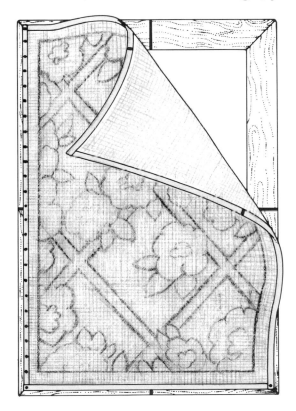

ing each pin (tack) opposite the other in tandem. This way you will be able to pull the canvas as taut as you can while distorting the weave as little as possible.

A scroll frame is a slightly more complex piece of equipment, but it has the advantage of being adjustable, which means that it is suitable for canvases of varying sizes. Instead of being attached directly to the frame itself, the canvas edges are sewn to the webbing on the horizontal rollers; then laced to the side laths, which will have pegs or screws for adjusting the dimensions and ensuring a good taut canvas to work on.

TO BLOCK A PIECE OF CANVASWORK

When all the stitching is complete, the piece of embroidery must first be blocked, or stretched, before it is made up into the finished article. Even if it has been worked on a frame and is not distorted, it will look fresher after blocking; and if it has been pulled out of shape, blocking is essential.

You will need a piece of plywood or hardwood at least 5cm (2 inches) larger all round than the work, a hammer, carpet tacks and the piece of blotting paper on which you have previously drawn the outline of the canvas. (If you have neglected to do this, draw a rectangle using two adjacent sides of the canvas as a guide to the measurements.)

Hold the work up to a strong light to make sure that no stitches are missing. Trim the thread ends closely on the wrong side. Clip the selvedge, if any, at short intervals; do not remove the masking tape or seam binding.

Tape the blotting paper to the board, and place the embroidery, wrong side up, on the board (first moistening it slightly if it is badly distorted). Tack it to the drawn outline at each corner. Continue tacking along all four sides, inserting the tacks at intervals of about 2cm (¾ inch).

Dampen the work thoroughly, using either a sponge or a spray bottle. For most types of work you should now leave it to dry thoroughly – this may take several days for something as large and thick as a rug. But in certain circumstances the canvas should be removed from the board while still damp, in which case instructions for this will be given under the individual design.

BASIC STITCHING TECHNIQUES

To start work, make a knot in the thread, and take the needle from the right side to the wrong side, a short distance ahead of the starting point. Bring the thread up at the starting point, then stitch until you reach the knot, which you can then cut off. To end the work, take the needle through the underside of a few stitches, then cut off the tail end of the yarn. A new thread can also be fastened by taking it through the wrong side of the stitches.

Canvas embroidery can be worked with either a 'sewing' or a 'stabbing' movement – unless, of course, the work is framed, in which case the stabbing movement must be used.

If you are left-handed, you may wish to reverse the direction of working shown in these diagrams. If you use the stabbing technique, you should be able to work comfortably in any direction; otherwise you will need to rotate the work in order to sew from right to left where necessary.

Avoid using too long a thread. About 50cm (20 inches) is the recommended maximum length. If the yarn becomes untwisted or kinks up, allow the needle to hang freely, and the yarn will resume its natural twist.

As a general rule, avoid bringing the needle up through a hole already partially filled with yarn.

The needle will tend to split the strands, producing an untidy effect. Working down into the hole smooths the fibres and makes the stitches more clearly defined.

STITCHES

There are many canvaswork stitches, but by far the most popular is continental tent stitch, which is also called petit point. This is worked over a single canvas thread intersection and is thus capable of depicting fine detail and subtle shading.

There are two forms of what might be called 'orthodox' tent stitch: continental tent stitch and basketweave tent stitch. Both of these produce a very firm fabric.

Half-cross stitch is virtually indistinguishable from basketweave and continental on the right side, but the resulting fabric is not so hard-wearing. It is probably the best method for a beginner to start with.

TENT STITCH (CONTINENTAL)

This stitch, which covers one mesh of the canvas, may be worked either horizontally or vertically. It is best to fasten off the thread at the end of a row, or take it through to the underside of the work, and work all rows in the same direction, rather than rotating the canvas on alternate rows, which would entail bringing up the needle through a previously-worked stitch. Because this stitch tends to distort the canvas, it should be worked on a frame.

TENT STITCH (BASKETWEAVE)

This version of tent stitch is worked diagonally. It has two main advantages over continental stitch: it hardly distorts the canvas at all, and rows are worked back and forth, without having to turn the canvas or fasten off the thread. It also uses slightly less thread and is ideal for backgrounds.

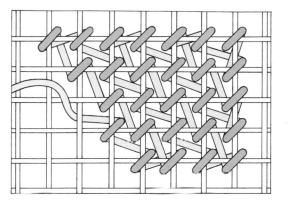

HALF CROSS STITCH

This stitch appears virtually identical to tent stitch on the right side, but covers only the horizontal thread of the canvas on the back. This makes it more economical on yarn but less firm. It is worked in rows, either horizontally or vertically. Take care not to pull the yarn too tightly. Half-cross must be worked on either interlock or double-thread canvas. Worked on single canvas, the stitches slip under the vertical threads. Half-cross can be worked back and forth; because the work is less dense than continental tent, the previously worked stitch is less likely to be disturbed.

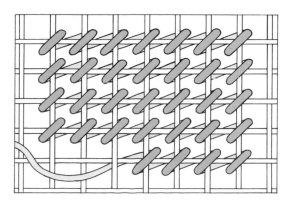

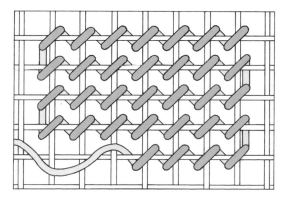

MAKING UP A SIMPLE CUSHION COVER

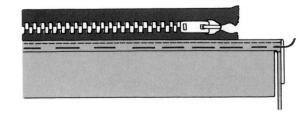

The inner cushion used should be the same size as the cover, or perhaps a little larger; this will ensure a good, plump fit, especially at the corners, which tend to wrinkle if a smaller pad (pillow form) is used.

The simplest way of making up a cushion is to place the embroidery and the backing fabric together with right sides facing, and stitch around three sides and part of the fourth, leaving a gap just large enough for inserting the pad. Then turn the cover right side out, insert the pad, and slipstitch the canvas edges together.

INSERTING A ZIP FASTENER

If you wish the cover to be removable, you can insert a zip in the backing fabric.

Cut two pieces of backing fabric, making each piece the height of the finished cover and half the width, plus 2cm (¾ inch) seam allowance on all edges.

Pin the two pieces together (with right sides facing) along one vertical edge. Stitch at either end, taking a 2cm (¾ inch) seam allowance and leaving a gap 2cm (¾ inch) longer than the zip; then tack (baste) with small stitches (or the longest machine stitch) along the zip opening. Press the seam open.

Turn under and press 5mm (¼ inch) on the seam allowance of one piece. Place this along the edge of the zip as shown, with the slider 1.5cm (½ inch) below the top of the tacking, the pull tab extended, and all the fabric lying to the right. Pin and tack (baste) through the fold of fabric and the zip.

Stitch by machine, using a zipper foot, or by hand, using a small, spaced backstitch, close to the edge of the fold.

Place the fabric right side up and opened out, with the zip lying flat underneath and with the pull tab turned down. Pin and tack (baste) along the re-maining edges of the zip, through all layers. Stitch by hand using backstitch, or by machine. Remove all tacking (basting), including the stitches holding the opening together.

When making up the cover, open the zip first and stitch around all four edges. Turn the cover right side out through the zip opening then insert the cushion pad (pillow form).

PIPING

A piped edge gives a cushion a professional-looking finish and is well worth the small amount of extra work.

Buy enough piping cord to go around the edges of the cushion, plus a little extra for joining. The fabric used is normally the same as that used for the back of the cushion. Avoid very thick fabrics and those that fray easily. For best results the strips should be cut on the bias (at a 45-degree angle to the selvedge).

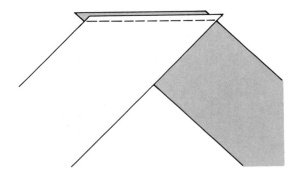

Cut strips of fabric, making the width equal to the circumference of the piping cord plus twice the seam allowance. Join strips, if necessary, on the straight grain, as shown above.

Wrap the strip around the cord, right side outside, and machine stitch close to the cord, using a zipper foot.

Pin then tack (baste) the piping to the back of the cushion cover, placing the cord inside the seamline, so that the seam allowances lie towards the edge. Clip the piping seam allowances at the corners to make them lie flat.

If the piping is narrow, the ends may simply be overlapped and tapered into the seam. If the piping is thick, end the tacking (basting) about 5cm (2 inches) to either side of the chosen joining point and unpick the stitching for the same distance. Join the fabric ends on the straight grain as described above; trim and press the seam. Cut the cord so that the ends overlap by 2-3cm (about 1 inch). Cut away two strands from one end and one from the other; wind the remaining strands together and bind them with thread. Fold the fabric over the cord and tack (baste) it in place.

Stitch the piping in place, just outside the seamline. Tack (baste) the back of the cover over the front, right sides facing, enclosing the piping. Stitch it in place, using the zipper foot, working as close as possible to the cord. Leave a gap for turning, unless a zip fastener has been inserted in the back.

MOUNTING EMBROIDERY FOR A PANEL

The method described here can be used for a panel (which should then be framed professionally) or for any other flat object, such as a box lid. You will need a piece of thick, acid-free cardboard or hardboard slightly larger (if for a panel) than the finished work. If the margin is to fit under the rebate of a frame moulding, it is best to select the moulding and measure the depth of the rebate before cutting the board. If in doubt, make the margin scant, as an overlap is obviously preferable to a line of unworked canvas. You will also need some large pins and strong thread.

Place the work right side down, and lay the board on top of it. Fold down one long edge of the canvas and pin it to the edge of the board at short intervals, leaving the required margin on the right side of the work. Repeat on the other long edge.

Thread a large needle with the strong thread, without cutting it from the reel (spool). Starting at the centre, lace the two edges together as shown, working through them alternately. Fasten the thread at one end. Cut off a generous length from the reel, and work to the opposite end. Before fastening off, pull the stitches firmly along the whole length to make sure the work is taut, and check that the margins of unworked canvas are equal. Fasten off and remove the panel pins or thumbtacks.

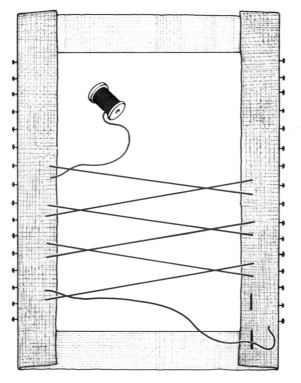

Repeat the lacing process on the remaining edges, folding the corner neatly.

Alternatively, the completed embroidery can be mounted on an artist's stretcher frame, as described on page 111.

YARN AND KIT INFORMATION

For the designs charted in this book it is best, although not essential, to use the yarns specified. Quantities have been calculated to allow for either half-cross, tent or basketweave stitch. As a result those using half-cross stitch will find that the amounts recommended will err on the generous side. This is preferable to having readers running out of colours and, as no two stitchers use exactly the same tension, quantities have purposely been estimated to allow room for this, and for wastage caused by mistakes. The yarns used in the canvaswork instructions given in this book – Anchor, Appleton and Rowan – are widely available in needlework shops. For information on your local stockist and mail-order sources contact the addresses below. All of the designs in the book (pictured on the following pages) are available as kits from Ehrman.

TAPESTRY WOOLS

Anchor Tapisserie: Coats Leisure Crafts Group, 39 Durham Street, Glasgow, Scotland G41 1BS. Tel: (041) 427 5311.
Susan Bates Inc., PO Box E, Route 9A, 212 Middlesex Avenue, Chester, Connecticut 06412, U.S.A. Tel: (203) 526 5381.

Appleton Bros. Ltd.: Thames Works, Church Street, Chiswick, London W4 2PE, England. Tel: (01) 994 0711.
American Creweland Canvas Studio, P.O. Box 453, 164 Canal Street, Canastota, NY 13032, U.S.A. Tel: (315) 697 3759.

Rowan Yarns Ltd.: Green Lane Mill, Holmfirth, West Yorkshire HD7 1RW, England. Tel: (0484) 681881.
The Westminster Trading Corporation, 5 Northern Boulevard, Amherst, NH 03031, U.S.A. Tel: (603) 886 5041.

EHRMAN

U.K.: Ehrman, 21/22 Vicarage Gate, London W8 4AA, England. Tel: (01) 937 4568.

U.S.A.: Ehrman, 5 Northern Boulevard, Amherst, NH 03031. Tel: (603) 886 5041.

Australia: Sunspun Enterprises PTY Ltd., 195 Canterbury Road, Canterbury, Victoria 3126. Tel: (03) 830 1609.

New Zealand: Quality Handcrafts, PO Box 1486, Auckland.

France: Armada, Collonge, Lournand, 71250 Cluny. Tel: 85 59 1356.

Canada: Estelle Designs and Sales Ltd., 38 Continental Place, Scarborough, Ontario M1R 2TA. Tel: (416) 298 9922.

Sweden: T.I.D.A., Box 2055, S-103 12 Stockholm. Tel: (468) 103355.

Italy: Sybilla S.r.l., Via Rizzoli 7, 40125 Bologna. Tel: (051) 750 875.

EHRMAN KITS

All of the canvaswork embroideries featured in this book are available as kits. The dimensions and the canvas mesh size for each embroidery are given below. All of the kits are suitable as cushions or pictures unless otherwise stated. To order kits contact Ehrman (addresses above).
Note: The Pheasant, Rabbit, Squirrel, Lurcher, Falcon and Monkey from the Hunting Rug by Candace Bahouth are all available as separate cushion designs using 7-mesh rug canvas and measuring 40×40cm (15½×15½in).

Embroiderers' Guild Squirrel
by Judith Gussin
38×38cm (15×15in),
12-mesh canvas

Griffin
by Judith Gussin
38×39cm (15×15½in),
12-mesh canvas

Cherub and Lion Hanging
by Lucinda Ganderton
95×74cm (37½×29in),
10-mesh canvas

Hunting Rug by Candace Bahouth (see Note above)
100×141cm (39½×55½in) 7-mesh rug canvas

Doves and Fruit Panel
by Margaret Murton
99×99cm (39×39in),
10-mesh canvas

Elephants and Warriors
by Anita Gunnett
43×43cm (16¾×16¾in),
12-mesh canvas

Labrador
by Catherine Reurs
36×36cm (14×14in),
12-mesh canvas

English Setter
by Catherine Reurs
36×36cm (14×14in),
12-mesh canvas

Parakeet and Pineapple
by Sue Rangeley
46×46cm (18×18in),
10-mesh canvas

Noah's Ark
by Catherine Reurs
47×47cm (18½×18½in),
12-mesh canvas

Pansy the Cow
by Kaffe Fassett
37×37cm (14¾×14¾in),
10-mesh canvas

Sheep at Cwmcarvan
by Sarah Windrum
37×35cm (14½×13½in),
12-mesh canvas

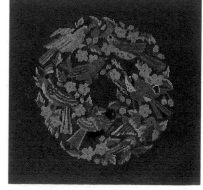

Two Elephants
by Marion Beatty for the Royal
School of Needlework
37×37cm (14½×14½in),
12-mesh canvas

Doves and Dovecote
by Joy Hanington
36×36cm (14×14in),
10-mesh canvas

Guatemalan Birds
by Susan Duckworth
35×34cm (13¾×13½in),
12-mesh canvas

Ring of Birds Chairseat
by Nancy Kimmins for the
Embroiderers' Guild
30cm (12in) diameter,
12-mesh canvas

Medieval Fantasy Stool
by Margaret Murton
43×33cm (17×13in),
14-mesh canvas

Canadian Goose
adapted by Ehrman
37×30cm (14½×12in),
12-mesh canvas

Victorian Cats
by Kaffe Fassett
43×32cm (17×12½in),
10-mesh canvas

Gloucestershire Pheasant
by Ann Blockley
37×37cm (14¾×14¾in,)
10-mesh canvas

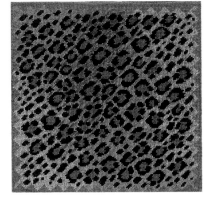

Leopardskin Cushion
by Candace Bahouth
38×38cm (15×15in),
12-mesh canvas

Cow Jumped over the Moon
by Julie Arkell
46×46cm (18×18in),
10-mesh canvas

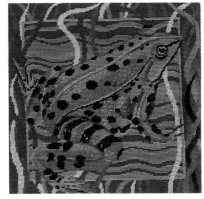

Frog in Reeds
by Angela Chidgey
40×40cm (15½×15½in),
10-mesh canvas

African Fish
by Lillian Delevoryas
43×43cm (17×17in),
10-mesh canvas

Pandas
by Lillian Delevoryas
36×36cm (14×14in),
10-mesh canvas

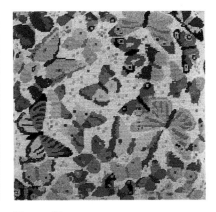

Butterflies
by Susan Duckworth
32×33cm (12¾×13in),
14-mesh canvas

Pink Cat
by Sarah Windrum
35.5×36cm (14×14¼in),
12-mesh canvas

Tigers
by Sue Rangeley
64×25cm (25×10in),
10-mesh canvas

BIBLIOGRAPHY

English Naïve Painting 1750-1900, James Ayres, Thames and Hudson, 1980

American Folk Art: Expressions of a New Spirit, Dr Robert Bishop, Museum of American Folk Art, 1982

Animals and Men, Kenneth Clark, Thames and Hudson, 1977

Twentieth-Century Embroidery in Great Britain (three volumes), Constance Howard, B. T. Batsford 1981-4

The Treasure Houses of Britain, ed. Gervase Jackson-Stops, National Gallery of Art, Washington, Yale University Press, 1985

Discovering Embroidery of the 19th Century, Santina Levey, Shire Publications, 1971 and 1977

The Flowering of American Folk Art, 1776-1876, Jean Lipman and Alice Winchester, Viking Press and The Whitney Museum of American Art, 1974

Victorian Embroidery, Barbara Morris, Herbert Jenkins, 1962

Textiles of the Arts and Crafts Movement, Linda Parry, Board of the Trustees of the Victoria and Albert Museum, and Thames and Hudson, 1988

Labours of Love: America's Textiles and Needlework, 1650-1930, Judith Reiter Weissman and Wendy Lavitt, Studio Vista, 1988

Needlework: An Historical Survey, ed. Betty Ring, Main Street Press, Pittstown, 1984

Figures on Fabric, Margaret Swain, A. & C. Black, 1980

The Needlework of Mary Queen of Scots, Margaret Swain, Van Nostrand Reinhold Company, 1973

Antique Needlework, Lanto Synge, Blandford Press, 1982

ACKNOWLEDGEMENTS

The following contributions shall not go unrecorded:

First and foremost Gillian Meakin at William Briggs and Co. who has turned original artwork for all these designs into workable models. This job requires great sensitivity, and I know I can speak for all the designers in congratulating her on the way she has dealt with their work.

Jean Stanley at the Readicut Wool Company, who originated the artwork for the Hunting Rug with equal skill.

Valerie Buckingham at Century Hutchinson who has expertly coordinated the production of this book.

Sue Storey and Patrick McLeavey for designing the book.

Julie Fisher for her wonderful photography and Jackie Boase for her most creative styling.

Eleanor Van Zandt and Sally Harding for advice on stitching, stretching and completing the tapestries.

Sue Breuilly and Carole Keegan at our office for critical and practical assistance throughout.

And finally, I would particularly like to thank Gail Rebuck and Sarah Wallace at Century who commissioned the book and have had the faith and confidence to allow it to evolve in the unpredictable and idiosyncratic way that it has!

PHOTO CREDITS

The publishers and authors would like to thank the following for permission to use illustrations:
The American Museum in Britain page 58; Ashmolean Museum, Oxford p.29; Candace Bahouth p.106; The Burrell Collection, Glasgow Museums & Art Galleries p.11; Christie's p.46; Embroiderers' Guild p.24 (photo Dudley Moss), p.94, p.98, p.102 (all Elizabeth Benn); Iona Antiques, London p.56; Mr P. Maxwell Stuart of Traquair p.20 (photo Martin Gostelow), Museum of English Naïve Art p.50; National Gallery of Ireland p.79; National Museum of Wales (Welsh Folk Museum) p.66; National Trust Photographic Library p.37; Newman & Cooling Ltd p.74; Duke of Northumberland p.38; Private Collection p.70; Sotheby's p.87; The Suffolk Collection, Ranger's House, Blackheath (English Heritage) p.19; Board of Trustees of the Victoria and Albert Museum p.22, p.23, p.47, p.55 (photo Ken Jackson), p.82, p.90, p.93; Whitworth Art Gallery, University of Manchester p.28; The Earl of Yarborough (Brocklesby Park) p.42.

LOCATION ACKNOWLEDGEMENTS

For the Hunting Rug and Rabbit, Squirrel and Lurcher cushions (Candace Bahouth); the Griffin and Squirrel cushions (Judith Gussin); the Ring of Birds chairseat (Nancy Kimmins for the Embroiderers' Guild); the Gloucestershire Pheasant cushion (Ann Blockley) and the Pink Cat cushion (Sarah Windrum) thanks to Dennis Severs, 18 Folgate Street, London E1 (tel. 01-247 4013).

For the Parakeet and Pineapple cushion and Tigers panel (Sue Rangeley); Elephants and Warriors cushion (Anita Gunnett) and the Two Elephants cushion (Royal School of Needlework) thanks to Christopher Farr Handmade Rugs, 115 Regents Park Road, London NW1 8UR (tel. 01-586 9684).

For the Leopardskin cushion (Candace Bahouth) thanks to Pacific Design, Zone 306, Business Design Centre, London N1 0QH (tel. 01-288 6156).

For providing and framing the Medieval Fantasy stool top (Margaret Murton) thanks to the Royal School of Needlework.

INDEX

Page references in italics denote illustrations and captions.